Too Far From Perfect:
A father-daughter conversation about public education

© **2013**

All rights reserved.
Published in Canada by Tai Pascal Notar and Charles E. Pascal

Publishers: Tai Pascal Notar and Charles E. Pascal

Too Far From Perfect: A father-daughter conversation about public education

ISBN: 978-0-9919727-1-5 [print], 978-0-9919727-0-8 [digital]

Cover photo: Dreamstime photo illustration
Book design & digital development: WildElement.ca

Too Far From Perfect:
A father-daughter conversation about public education

TAI PASCAL NOTAR & CHARLES E. PASCAL

Contents

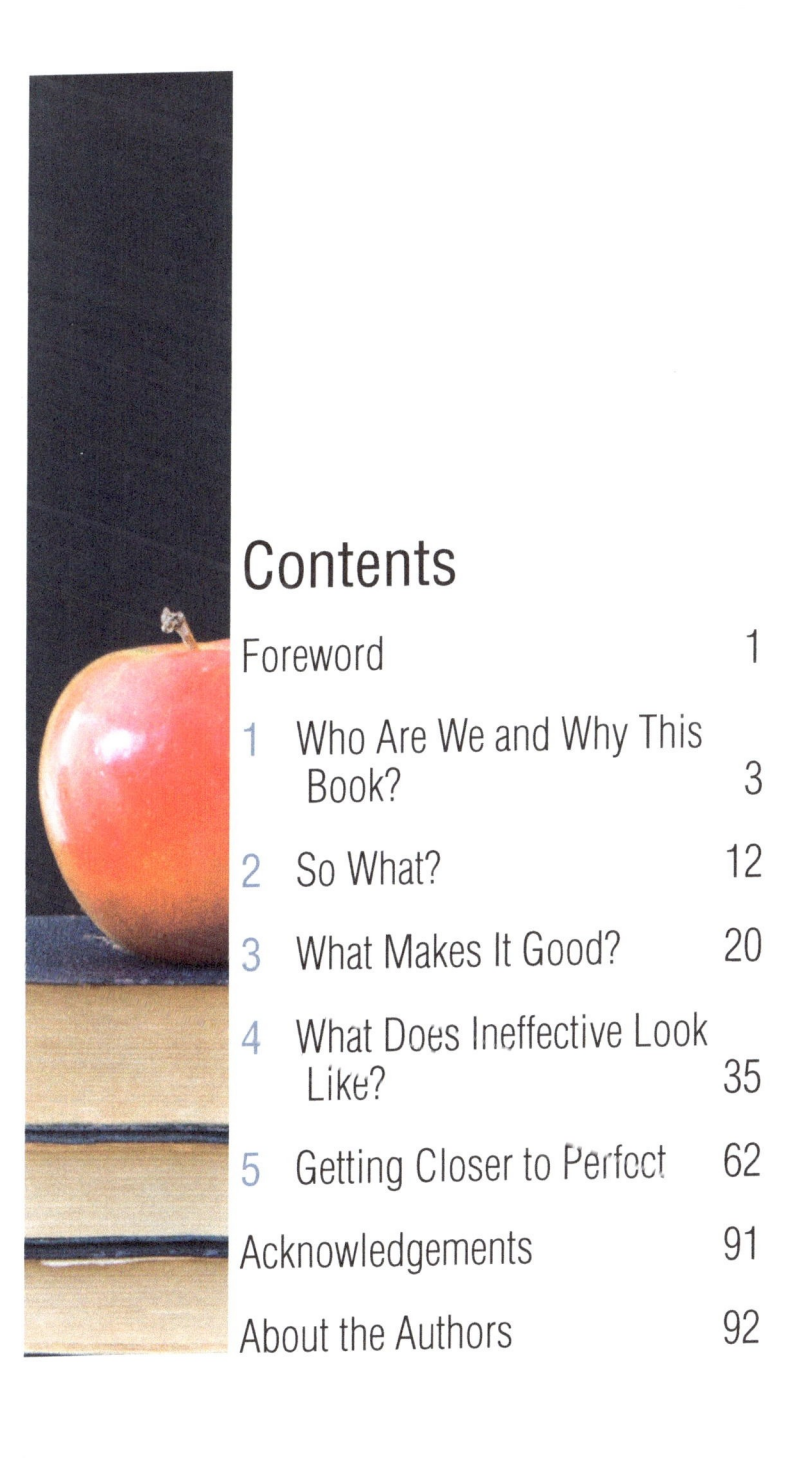

Foreword		1
1	Who Are We and Why This Book?	3
2	So What?	12
3	What Makes It Good?	20
4	What Does Ineffective Look Like?	35
5	Getting Closer to Perfect	62
Acknowledgements		91
About the Authors		92

We dedicate this book to our kids/brothers/sisters/ grandkids/nieces/nephews who create many interesting and important opportunities for us to learn new, exciting and unexpected things.

Foreword

Take an aware 4 year old in early learning who becomes increasingly perceptive about her schooling experiences over the next 13 years into grade 12; add an inquisitive, caring father who happens to be an expert in early learning and higher education. Listen in as they discuss just about everything having to do with daily experiences in the school. What you have is Tai and Charles—daughter and dad dissecting the challenges of the learning experience in pubic education. What you have is *Too Far from Perfect*.

It's a personal journey for sure. But it works as a kind of micro account of what it's like to be a student in a big system, and a parent whose instincts are to be more interventionist than he knows he should be. Through the natural conversations that flow from "how was school today", we find out how the little things are in fact *big* in their consequences—for better or for worse.

We learn a good deal. We learn how students have much to offer by way of constructive feedback to teachers under the right circumstances. We learn that they are much more insightful, and sensitive—not only to the needs of their peers but also the circumstances of the teacher—than is commonly recognized. We see unveiled a deep underutilized resource that would be easy to tap into and would have great benefits for the lives of students and teachers working more collaboratively. All of this is at the micro level; any student, parent, teacher would gain a great deal if they read this personal account and reflected on it in relation to their own experiences. I guarantee you that you will recognize some of your selves, and that you will open up avenues of thought that were in you, but unrecognized and untapped. You will discover things that you never thought about that are at first personal but on reflection generalizable.

While this is a personal journal of just two people, it feels familiar. We see ourselves as students recalling those teachers that have faded from memory—for some, good riddance, for others, the memory of a teacher who may have turned your life around is indelible. While these personal connections stoke memories, the reader gradually gets introduced into bigger policy matters. How should teachers be selected; what are the relative roles of academic knowledge, and emotional intelligence; what can a student do if the teacher is not listening; what is the role of the principal in relation to improving teachers individually, and especially in helping them learn together. How can policy improve teachers and teaching, and what should the role of the student be, not as a recipient of knowledge but as a learning partner.

Too far from Perfect makes you think in an enjoyable and insightful way. It is a learning journey. You can be inside the lives of Tai and Charles, and at the same time inside your own life. And you can wonder what it is like for the thousands of other families you know and don't know. You can improve things if you take some action based on your reflections. Read it to stimulate your imagination—treat it as equivalent to taking a shower to let creative ideas come from the unconscious realm that is in you, but not yet surfaced. Enjoy the book. Learn from it. Act on it.

— Michael Fullan, OC.
 Professor Emeritus, OISE, University of Toronto

1 Who Are We and Why This Book?

My name is Tai Notar. I'm like most Grade 12 kids; I have had about 60 teachers since kindergarten. With all this experience with teachers, I've come to understand how great teachers can make a difference. I've been really lucky. Many of mine have been amazing but there have been too many who were not.

I was eight years old when I met Madame R in Grade 2. She was the first teacher I can remember who made a noticeable difference in my life. She taught me the lesson of kindness when she made a fresh pot of tea for a classmate to soothe his sore throat. She used her own mini-zoo to teach us respect and to reward us for good work and responsibility. What a wonderful collection of little animals that we were allowed to play with in that classroom. We were even encouraged to take care of them which was a great treat for me because I love animals. Madame R gave me an early understanding of the importance of having a good teacher. She wasn't just a teacher; she was a role model that everyone could aspire to be.

I also had Madame R in Grade 3. Over the course of this year, she came to suspect that I had some kind of learning disability. It turned out she was right. I got tested and as a result, I learned more about myself and that I needed to learn in different ways. This has made a huge difference in my life. I went from being a kid who didn't understand why I was getting Cs to figuring out how to learn differently so that I could be a regular on the honours list. Without Madame R's observation, Dad and I wouldn't be doing this book.

My Grade 7 teacher taught me not to always trust first impressions. Mr. A was pretty serious on the first day of class, listing all of the class rules. It turned out he was a funny, friendly, caring guy who couldn't do enough to help. He came in early for one-on-one meetings to help kids like me overcome struggles with Math even though he wasn't our math teacher. His after-school soccer coaching was another way for him to help kids learn because it gave him another way to establish trust, with opportunities to get some students to listen more carefully to what he was saying. He made us laugh with stories from his own life and jokes at his own expense that still make me laugh. His classroom was a place full of joy, a very enjoyable place to learn.

I'll never forget Ms. M, my Grade 8 homeroom teacher, who clearly hadn't stopped learning herself. She was always experimenting and always reading about new things to try out, such as our preferred learning styles. Turns out I am a kinesthetic, logical, musical learner. I have learned that I like doing off-the-wall things, connecting old things in new ways. I also like hands-on problem-solving.

I guess that's why I decided on a high school that emphasizes creativity, and that has amazing dance, music, and art teachers. But creative teaching is not limited to the arts; many who teach English, math and science are incredibly inventive as well. I have had such encouragement that I am now far more confident performing in front of the class and doing assignments with an outside-the-box approach because I feel my school is a safe environment in which I can take risks.

I have also learned that school principals matter. I had a great Grade 9 math teacher, Mr. L. who ran an after-school math group to assist our learning. To my surprise and delight

Mr. S, our principal, was there too, to support us and to broaden his learning as well. He ended up being there every Tuesday He led by example, not just by words. That's what great teachers are — great leaders who inspire us, make us feel like following them and make us want to pay attention to what they have to offer. A good example of this is Mr. E, my Grade 9 geography teacher who asked us on the first day of class: "What does NOT have anything to do with geography?" We had to try to stump him and couldn't. His point? To connect the subject of geography with our world and our interests, Mr. E led me down a path of enjoyment and I learned that geography is much more than it seems.

I have had many other fantastic teachers. I am grateful for the teachers who seem happy to be with us students and who are genuinely interested in us. The good ones seem really pleased to be teaching and content with their lives in general. They are interested in their subjects and they continue to be learners who are more excited about what they don't know as they teach us what they do know.

I am fortunate to have had many opportunities to learn outside of school and this has also helped to give me a good sense of what works for me. I love to ride horses and my riding coach is amazing. I do a lot of extra-curricular training in voice and dance and have had some great instructors. I have also spent a lot of time volunteering.

I feel that my own experiences are good examples of what education can be both inside and outside school.

While I have been lucky so far, I have also learned that, there are too many teachers who are not helpful. They turn students off subjects or even off learning altogether. As well, there are things that get in the way of student learning that are not the fault of the teachers but part of the larger school-board system.

I think most teachers do want to do the right things and

many know how, but too many don't. If you add up the amount of wasted time and chances to learn that arise from from poorly trained or un-motivated teachers and substitute teachers in a school year, we are probably talking of more than a day a week of lost opportunities.

These teachers need help and support. They deserve it and, while some may not want it, we need to figure out how to create an environment where they would be more open to improving their teaching. Students can be a key part of this. . It is important that we do all we can to make education great for all kids and not make anyone feel badly about things that aren't working.

I believe that everyone has a role in improving education. Students and parents have an obligation to do their part — to make sure that students are putting in the effort that's necessary to do well — but the emphasis of this book is on what the education system's role is and what it needs to do to help more students succeed and be excited about learning.

There are many good things I have experienced in my schooling but education as I know it is far from perfect and it must be improved. My dad and I often share stories about all of this and this book is a conversation between us that offers some ideas to help get education closer to perfect.

Tai Pascal Notar (Courtesy the author)

I'm the dad, Charles E. Pascal. I love to learn, love to help others learn and I agree with Tai that there are many things right with education in Canada today but education in our country is too far from perfect. I have been an educator for most of my adult life, whatever "adult life" actually means. But chronologically and formally speaking, I have taught at the university level since I was 22 years old — over forty years of trying to figure out how best to enable the learning of my students. Learning to listen carefully to Tai's stories and trying to mine the gold from her experience has been the single most important professional development I have had thus far.

My earliest memory of formal schooling takes me back to my first day in kindergarten at Clinton Public School on the North Side of Chicago. It was one of the most memorable days of my life, and likely one of the worst and most traumatic. While I don't remember why Miss A wrapped a roll or two of scotch tape around my mouth and put me in a closet half way through the morning, it just might be that the behaviour of a five year old is a pretty good predictor of what's ahead. My curiosity and my rather outgoing personality and confidence about expressing myself were probably at play that morning many decades ago.

Putting in me in a closet, however, with my mouth wrapped as an early Christmas present to the quiet god was a touch extreme. If you are a fan of the Wizard of Oz, picture the wicked witch and you can conjure up Miss A.

I went home and told my mother, "I am never ever going to school again!" With a phone call to the principal and my father's firm and friendly "request," I gave public education one more chance. Glad I did. On day two I was escorted into Miss M's class. If Miss A was the wicked witch, Miss M was the nice witch of the north. She immediately recognized my leadership skills and put me in charge of cleaning out the hamster cage, and I had my first real crush. On Miss M, not the hamster!

So I gave school a try but was bored in the extreme in Grades 1 and 2. Until Grade 3, I spent more time with the vice-principal than I did with my teachers.

Then I met Miss P. She made a real difference for me in the classroom and beyond; she might have even saved my life. She cared enough about my journey to take an interest in seeing me move from a hyperactive and mischievous kid to a highly motivated learner. She made a magical thing happen in my life by showing me that getting through a day in the classroom and being creative and having fun were not incompatible ideas. She took me, an extreme version of the class clown, and tapped into my assets, the stuff I enjoyed. Before I knew it, I was a peer tutor for other kids and was allowed to do all of my assignments using my love of baseball in my work. She understood one of fundamental aspects of great pedagogy — the ability to adapt to the individual differences of students.

For me it was the end of suspensions from school and the beginning of a love of learning that's still going strong.

As Tai noted, the idea for this book springs from her almost daily response to my "so how was school today" query. I am not sure why Tai is such a perceptive consumer of education but I have been constantly struck by the quality of her reporting, her analysis of the good and her concerns and insights about what's just not right or effective.

As a parent, I have heaped praise on the teachers who have made a difference for her and I have acted as an advocate on her behalf when things have not gone so well when she was younger. As she progressed in school, I have also tried to support her need for self-advocacy and she has done well, notwithstanding that providing constructive criticism to a teacher is very tricky business for a student.

The aim of this book, our conversation, is to underscore the critical importance for parents to listen to their kids' student experience, and to reinforce with teachers how critically important it is for them to listen to students. Teachers need to hear about how things are working for their students and ensure that students feel that this feedback will be actively sought, received and acted upon by all educators. The great ones know this. But most of us educators aren't superstars. We're average or above, seeking to be great.

In the final analysis, no matter how we define "quality education", it is the teacher who is key to enabling the learning of our kids. I come to this discussion, like Tai, with a huge respect for teachers. With increased diversity and complexities within the job, many teachers are doing very well, often under difficult circumstances. But as Tai has said, there is big room for improvement.

But improvement can be an enemy of the changes we need because making improvements here and there usually means working on the edges rather than making fundamental shifts regarding how things are done. And when we look at learning and the important role that teachers play, we would be myopic if we didn't pay attention to those who teach the teachers in the first place, those who lead teachers in the schools, and the external issues that get in the way of teachers being able to do their best.

Tai and I want to explore these things through the observations she has made, the stories she has to tell.

Experts make a big deal about getting kids ready for school. We need to do better at getting schools ready for kids. We hope our conversation will encourage other students and parents to share their stories with educators and we hope more educators will go out of their way to seek and act upon the issues revealed in these narratives. I agree with Tai: our aim is to provide positive ideas about making things better for all kids.

To paraphrase the late leadership guru, Stephen Covey, we want educators to seek to understand their students before seeking to be understood.

Finally, a note about authorship. Most of this book is Tai's narrative, her stories. From time to time, I replace my dad's hat with my expert's hat; but that doesn't happen often because Tai usually doesn't let me get away with playing the "professor". . . . These are conversations poured onto the page and refined through my listening and questioning. Tai and I then spent considerable time ensuring that our voices are clear in tone, content and authenticity.

Charles E. Pascal (Courtesy the author)

2 So What?

Charles: Let's begin with the obvious question: Why is public education so important, Tai?

Tai: Dad, It's obvious to me that education improves peoples' lives — at least it's supposed to. You know, we will have a better society and more opportunities for people. People will do more of the right things. There will be less crime, less poverty and things like that.

Charles: You say, "supposed to" improve lives. You sound skeptical.

Tai: That's the point of this book, isn't it? If education is talked about as the best thing ever for a society, then why do so many kids fail, get turned off learning, drop out, learn to hate French or math or science? Why do we have so many substitute teachers? Why do so many of them know nothing about the subject? Why are so many regular teachers disrespectful to students? Why are so many of them not trained in the subjects they are supposed to be teaching? Aren't those who are teaching the teachers making sure that anyone who graduates with a teachers' education degree actually knows how to teach?

Charles: Geez, Tai, You have told me time and again that most of your teachers have been superstars. What gives?

Tai: That's actually true, Dad. I'm just saying that if education is so important, then the things that aren't working have some serious issues. Come on, you know that I was really good at French, better than you, right?

Charles: Okay, your French vocabulary and grammar are better than mine, but what's your point?

Tai: My point is simple. I was really enjoying French until Ms X arrived in my life. Her French was awful and her approach to teaching was worse. Yes, I got an A in the course but I learned to hate French. I would rather have received a B but learned to love French even more. I know that doesn't sound smart and that I should have continued my French, but that's how I felt. I have heard from too many of my friends that many French teachers are just not up to the job. So, if French is one of our two official languages, and education is so important, why is this allowed to happen as often as it does?

Charles: Okay, *Je comprends*. While I am not so sure the problem is as big as you say it is, I do understand that the emotional side of the experience was what led you to drop French. I certainly agree with your reasons why education is so important to society in general. But let's get personal. Why is it so important to you?

Tai: Well, I want to have a happy and healthy life and that means that I need to learn the kinds of things that will help me get that. I want to be able to understand things around me so I can feel confident about what to enjoy and what to change. That means learning about the environment, science, geography and civics, stuff like that. I want to be able to eventually have a job that I enjoy that gives me the money I need to support myself. That means math and communications and learning how to work in teams on projects. I want to develop my creativity — that would be good for all aspects of my life and that means learning more about the arts.

Charles: How's it working for you so far, Tai?

Tai: So far, really well but I am still interested in how to make things better for me and for other kids. Dad, I just don't see why some things are allowed to happen if education is so important. I believe that teachers and principals need to listen to us. We can help them. You know that I have been pretty good at advocating for myself and you have been there for me as well. But sometimes it's hard to be confident with some teachers because they have power over me and they kind of let you know they do.

Charles: Maybe I have been too involved as an advocate when the situations have required support; maybe your confidence would be even higher if I had stayed out of it. What do you think?

Tai: I disagree. More parents should get involved. When you have raised questions with teachers about a few things here and there and they responded positively, it showed me that most teachers want to be helpful and it gave me more confidence to take on things myself. Unfortunately, in talking with my friends, I think their parents are as scared about talking with teachers about how to improve things for their kids, as the kids are.

Charles: You really think so?

Tai: Yep. It makes me wonder if the education system is really as friendly as people make it seem to be. If parents are afraid to raise their voices, how can you expect students to? It's a tricky situation. As a parent, I imagine your worst fear is to make your child's life at school worse than it was before. As a student, I can tell you that my worst fear about speaking out is to give the teacher a reason to dislike me. Remember the situations that arose with the two team teachers in English who constantly told us different things and confused us all the time? Remember the time when each one told me completely opposite things about a word I used in a sentence in an essay?

Charles: I remember, of course I do, are you kidding? Come to think of it, that was about the fifth time that it turned out that I was the only parent to talk to the principal. I haven't been happy to hear principals say, "But no one else has complained about this," when in fact I thought others had. So far, every time you have told me a story that suggested something serious needed attention, you have been accurate. More recently, your self-advocacy has left me on the sidelines where I belong, cheering you on.

Tai: That's the point, and this is one of the reasons education is working for me. I am learning that although things are going well, it won't always be that way and there will be difficult situations that I will need to deal with. I need to decide if I can change something for the better, or whether I just need to get on with it. Or avoid it because I can't change the situation. But educators also need to be role models for the qualities that make society better, like kindness, respect and eagerness to learn new things.

Charles: Amen. Could it be that these are the most important lessons you are learning in school? How to work with other people with approaches both similar and different from yours; discovering how you like to learn; finding out about your passions; and how to communicate clearly in the right way at the right time. With education, I often say that the "process is the product." Did I ever tell you that the word "education" comes from the Latin word "educo," which means to "lead out from within." In other words, education is a process to find out what's inside you.

Tai: You're not giving a convocation address, Dad. Remember, we're having a conversation. But I get the point and agree with you. For me, there have been more positives about school than negatives, so the negatives are simply problems here and there that need to be solved. And yes, there is lots of learning that comes from this problem-solving. However, for way too many kids, there is more that's negative and the good things are here and there for them. They feel left out and ignored. They come to school with little confidence about being successful, and they leave with even less. If education is about making a better society, it needs to graded by how it helps every single kid.

Charles: So why are you so interested in making it better, not just for you, but for everyone? When do you think that you began to be so interested in learning, in education?

Tai: It goes back to my childcare experiences, I think. When did I start childcare?

On the way to lifelong learning (Shutterstock image)

Charles: Seems like yesterday. You were about 15 months old. Wobbly walk, very hesitant, holding my hand, squeezing my hand harder as I prepared to hand you over to strangers — two early childhood educators. You shed a few tears, and I kept hold of my tears until I was out of sight. A very emotional memory indeed. It was about the morning of day three that you broke my clasp and ran — or wobbled more quickly, but on your own — to the front door of the childcare centre, so excited about your new home away from home. And after a few more weeks, the end of the day pick-up was very difficult as I tried to pry you way from your play, learning beside other kids, still a few months shy of actually playing with other kids. In my opinion, this was the beginning of the joyful and confident lifelong learner that you are today.

Tai: I think most people know that we need to look at the bigger picture of education, that kids' experience before they get to school is really important.

Charles: Absolutely. That's why Ontario and so many other places around the world have understood the importance of early child education. You know in Ontario, 28% of children were showing up in Grade 1 well behind their peers before we implemented full-day learning for four- and five-year-old kids. It all really begins at birth. Parents and guardians are the first and most important teachers a child has. We need to improve ways to educate parents about some of the key things they can do to support their children's natural interests in learning. Reading to them, telling them stories, exposing them to music, creating wonderfully healthy play environments — because play is an incredible way to support and develop the natural curiosity kids are born with. Poverty doesn't help for sure. When kids need special supports, extra help beyond what the school can provide, parents with money can provide tutors. And the kids whose folks have resources are likely to have had computers in the home since they were quite young. So money can make a difference, unfortunately.

Tai:. That doesn't seem fair. Shouldn't the school provide the extra tutors and computers? I know I've been lucky. I have had some great extra help from my schools. But it's true, whenever ever I needed extra help, you and mom have supported me by doing what's been necessary, and I know some of that help has required money.

Charles: Yep, poverty is a big challenge but great public education is about making things more even, more equitable in the long run. The better one's education, the more likely one can "escape" poverty. Great public education can be the great equalizer. But did you know that 60% of those vulnerable kids showing up in Grade 1 are not poor? Vulnerable kids are those who are not doing well, and are well behind the other kids when it comes to learning.

Tai: So, is that why early learning is so important, the full-day kindergarten for four- and five-year-old kids?

Charles: Yes, we need better early-years support.

Tai: I guess great education is about making sure we know how to ask the right questions because we'll never know everything we need to know at every single point in our lives. And also about how to get answers that make sense ?

Charles: For sure! Things would be a lot better in the world if we all knew the right questions to ask at a given moment and knew how to gather a bit of evidence.

Tai: Hey, do you remember that kid from the United States we met on the train last year, the one who said President Obama wasn't an American, wasn't born in the U.S.?

Charles: I certainly won't forget that conversation, especially when she stated that Obama's middle name was "all one needed to know about him."

Tai: Yeah, her mother looked proud as she said that. Imagine, thinking that being a Muslim was a bad thing. The kid had never been in a class with kids with religions other than her own and Obama isn't even a Muslim.

Charles: That was the purest form of ignorance you will likely come across and that is what great public education is designed to overcome. But we need to better understand that kid's circumstances, her parents' upbringing, what's going on in her school and how different it is from yours. Learning to be more empathetic should also be a goal of education, you know, to put yourself in some else's shoes.

Tai: Yes! The importance of listening, paying close attention to the other person's situation.

Charles: And as you said before, teaching us all, kids and parents alike, to ask the right questions, and to seek good evidence, and to learn the lesson of respect and the joy of learning are all at the heart of effective public education.

Tai: For sure, which is why public education is so important, and worth the efforts to make it even better.

3 What Makes It Good?

Charles: Tai, you always talk about the great teachers you have had. What makes them so good?

Tai: Well, first of all, they are respectful. Most of my teachers have done all of the little things consistently. This consistency is important; it proves they are "real" about respect. After a class or two, they know my name and pronounce it correctly. It sounds simple but it sure makes me feel good to know they know me. My Grade 10 science teacher, Mr. L, had about thirty of us and by the end of the first class, he knew each of us by name.

Charles: Really? How did he do that?

Tai: Well, he had a seating chart but after he used that for half the class, he was calling on us by name without looking. At the end of the class, we quizzed him. We couldn't believe it. He called out our names forwards and backwards, pronounced all of our names correctly. It was amazing.

Charles: But obviously he has an extraordinary memory for names and faces.

Tai: Probably, but it doesn't matter. When a teacher sends out a signal that they are even trying to learn your name, she or he is letting us know that "I want to get to know you." This kind of teacher also shows interest in who we are as people, what we are like, what we like to do outside of their classes, because the more they know about us and the more they understand us, the teachers are able to adapt to our interests. For example, I can do some of my assignments where I use my own experience as examples for an assignment. If they show respect and display trust, it's like any relationship. It works. In the case of school, it just helps make me want to do well.

Charles: Maybe you could give me a few stories about teachers who have shown you respect. What did they do that gave you that sense other than knowing your name?

Tai: I think teachers show respect when they deal with who a person really is, taking into account both strengths and challenges. Do you remember when Mr. L, my Grade 9 math teacher gave me a chance to correct a silly mistake I made on a test?

Charles: No, I don't remember.

Tai: Well, I got the right answers for most of the test but for one part, there was a summary box where I was supposed to take each answer and put it in the box. I went too quickly over the instructions and failed to do that part.

Charles: One of your learning disability challenges — the need to carefully read the instructions, then review, then review again! So what happened?

Tai: I got a 70 on the test. But after class, Mr. L called me over, asked me to read the instruction I had not noticed and asked, " So now that you have read this again, what would you do?" He handed me my test and I took 30 seconds to record my answers in that box. He smiled and took my test back and handed it back to me with a big fat 85%!

Charles: So what's the lesson about respect?

Tai: He is a math teacher. He knew I had the right answers and he was trying to help me with other aspects of my learning challenges. I got the math part right but he was coaching me beyond the subject. I guess you could say he was educating all of me. The reason he could do that is because had made the effort to know me. That's respect.

Charles: Another example?

Tai: My Grade 10 science teacher, another Mr. L, discovered that I did pretty well on most of my science exams and quizzes, but he noticed that it was odd that I didn't do well on the multiple-choice parts. For most students, that's the easier part. Again, my reading challenges — my decoding problem — got in the way. So he spent time with me going over multiple-choice strategy, eliminating the silly answers. He also helped me learn some other strategies, and kept telling me to focus and review

Charles: So he was coaching all of you.

Tai: Yes, and he also gave extra time to some of us.

Charles: Is that fair for some kids to get extra time?

Tai: Why not? Some kids, like me, need extra time in some subjects. I usually finish earlier than other kids in English, history, and some other subjects but I need more time in subjects like math and science. I know the stuff, I just need more time.

Charles: You have hit on a very important point about one of the problems with the structure of our education system. Many years ago, a psychologist by the name of J.B.Carroll (1962, Model of School Learning), came to some conclusions about aptitude. Do you know what aptitude is?

Tai: Whether someone is good at something or not?

Charles: Exactly. That's how we commonly talk about aptitude — you have it or you don't. For example you have an aptitude for learning a dance routine and I don't. Carroll looked at it differently. He concluded through his research that aptitude is the different amount of time it takes different people to learn the same thing. So when you said before that you finish some tests earlier than others and other subjects require more time for you, that is exactly what Carroll was getting at. Carroll is saying it's not a question of good or bad. Remember, it's about the time it takes to learn something. You have some teachers who understand this and provide extra time to learn. And you have a right to this accommodation because you have a learning disability and this has led to your individualized education plan (IEP).

Tai: Does this mean that all teachers should provide all kids extra time in the subjects they aren't good at — or as you are saying, don't have a high aptitude for? Should all kids have an IEP?

Charles: Why not?

Tai: Well, eventually we would run out of time. The grades still have to be marked and recorded and report cards sent out when the semester or the school year is over. And what about students with really low aptitudes? No matter how much time they are given, they won't be able to pass.

Charles: Not necessarily. You are right about the pressure on teachers to get their marking done. They have time constraints, for sure. That's because of the current and traditional structure. So think about how the education system is organized. If Carroll's approach were applied, what would be different?

Tai: Well, everybody could get As.

Charles: Right! At least theoretically. Currently, we hold time constant. What I mean is, "It's June 15th, time's up. Tai, you get a B in this subject and your friend gets an A." We hold time constant and allow success in learning to vary.

Tai: I think I get it. If we care about kids' learning and their success, we would allow them the time they need, acknowledging that different kids learn different things at a different pace.

Charles: Exactly.

Tai: So, for this to work we would need another way to look at the school year. I wouldn't want to go to school all year long.

Charles: Well, speaking of going to school year round, ever wonder why we have two-month long summer breaks?

Tai: No.

Charles: Way back, well before my time, we used to have an agrarian economy when a majority of families were farmers. The two-month break gave these families the extra help that their kids could provide.

Tai: Really? But now farmers are in the minority right?

Charles: Exactly, but the school year remains the same.

Tai: So what's wrong with that?

Charles: Well, let's set aside the challenges of families trying to figure out how to arrange summers that balance out vacation time of parents with the two "free" months their kids have. From a learning perspective, a year round approach provides more continuity, greater capacity for dealing with those individual differences you talk about and less "learning loss" that can occur with a long break.

Tai: Ouch, going to school year round would not be very popular with students or teachers.

Charles: Yes, I get that and many teachers have other jobs during the summer and it's the same with students. And many businesses are organized to make money off of the two- month summer break. But there are countries that have this schedule and it works well. For example, Australia has a year round approach with four ten-week terms and two week breaks in between. They also have a year-end break that begins just before Christmas to the end of January-their summer vacation. This year round approach has the potential to provide for more learning momentum, better use of the school's physical resources, and easier planning for families for shorter breaks.

Tai: Will never happen here Dad!

Charles: Probably right Tai, but would be good to have

a discussion about it! But it's not just about the time issue. It's also about those other things you were talking about — the way effective teachers adapt their teaching to each student, their interests and their other ways of learning. Think about some of the other teachers who have had an impact on you.

Tai: I mentioned some of them in the introduction. One of the things that make a big difference is when students are permitted to get to know the teachers too. . . . That really helps to develop a trusting relationship.

Charles: So while it is important for them to know you, you are saying that the reverse is true as well. Why does it really matter? You're not expecting to be real friends with teachers, are you?

What makes a good teacher? (Dreamstime photo illustration)

Tai: No, but I feel that I can be the real me if I know the teacher as a person. I can take more risks, feel more confident to ask dumb questions, and admit I need help if don't understand something. Or I can ask the teacher if he or she would like me to assist with another student having trouble with a project.

Charles: Have you ever done that?

Tai: Yes, remember that situation with my friend who was afraid to ask her teacher for help and I acted as an advocate with the teacher? That would not have happened unless I felt comfortable with the teacher.

Charles: Does having a better and more real relationship with teachers mean that they will go easy on you?

Tai: You mean give me better grades?

Charles: Sure, or be more lenient with you about assignment deadlines.

Tai: Dad, you know I never miss a deadline. My problem is getting things done too quickly! But no, I don't expect an easy ride — that's not the point. Teachers who share some things about who they are, just get more respect in return, more understanding from their students.

Charles: Have you had a teacher who shared too much?

Tai: Yes, I had one teacher who seemed very needy. It seemed like he was in real need of friends and shared more than a bit too much. I am just not sure it's appropriate for us to know details about his love life. So I'm not talking about teachers getting overly personal with us.

Charles: Tai, can you think of some examples that illustrate the right balance?

Tai: Well, when we know if someone has kids, their ages, what their partners do if they are in a relationship — this makes them human to us. Almost all of the good teachers fill us in along the way. Sometimes, there is something quite significant about someone and they let us know upfront.

For example, my Grade 7 teacher, Ms. M, made it clear that she was gay on day one. She did this in a very low key way, but referred to her partner by her first name. It was no big deal but it was a nice way of saying, "This is who I am, who are you?" Do you remember the story that Mom's friend's son told about his Grade 11 teacher? After a few weeks of class, the teacher put the word "gay" on the board and asked kids to say words they associated with the word. Some kids said nice words, others mentioned stereotype words and phrases like "great dressers" and others yelled out some nasties. After five minutes of this, the teacher circled the work "gay" and wrote his name inside the circle. That was the end of lesson, but the beginning of an introduction about who he was.

Charles: I wonder if the kids who said some of the nasty things felt pretty badly when he came out to them.

Tai: They were a bit uncomfortable but the teacher played it "relaxed," no big deal and treated those students with kindness and respect. It was probably the last time they ever were negative about gays.

Charles: Any other things that the effective teachers do

Tai: Well, in addition to respecting us, understanding who we are and building on our strengths, they know how to make learning an active process. The really good teachers get us involved in solving problems through projects, even playing games and they create lots of opportunities for our curiosity to be aroused. Experiments are great, not only in science. I have had some English teachers who really know how to keep us actively turned on.

Charles: Tai, do you remember when we were discussing the power of play with very young children? Well, that's what you're talking about. Many people now understand that when a three or four year old is at a water table spilling water as she pours it from a large container into a smaller one, she is learning about important concepts, especially if a well-trained educator is there to ask a few simple questions.

Tai: So Dad, why do we stop this play-based stuff when we start Grade1?

Charles: We shouldn't. Teaching approaches that emphasize the kinds of things that you are talking about really work. Building on the interests and learning approaches that define students and allowing an active process of "testing" things and solving problems works regardless of age.

Tai: You know Dad, for me, how someone teaches is more important than what they teach!

Charles: Really, Tai? Don't you need to ensure you learn all that the Ontario curriculum intends you to learn?

Tai: Yeah, for sure. But remember Mr. E, my Grade 9 geography guy. He turned me on to geography big time and I took a course from him again in Grade 11. It wouldn't matter what he is teaching. I know I will learn tons of good things from him and so will all of the other students. I planned on taking Grade 12 Mr. E too. Doesn't matter what he is teaching. And I'm doing the same thing with other teachers, just taking the courses they teach now that I have more choices. In Grade11, I also went to a sample lecture of another Mr. L who teaches history and philosophy to get a sense of what he might be like. Wow, he was amazing, so I chose him for Grade 12 philosophy.

Charles: Come to think of it, that's the strategy I used in university when I had more choices as well. But you have switched out of a course after a week when the approach didn't match your learning style. Isn't that correct?

Tai: Yes, but only when I had enough information about another teacher I thought would be a better match for me.

Charles: So you do understand that often it's a question of a match between a student and teacher and not just a question of good or bad teaching.

Tai: Yes, for sure, but generally great teaching matches up with all students. That's the point I have been trying to make about understanding each student's interests and styles.

Charles: The ability to adapt to the individual differences of students! Remember when we were on vacation in Italy and we went to a town called Reggio Emilia?

Tai: Yeah, Mom and I went shopping and you went to some place about early learning.

Charles: Correct. This is a place where they have infant/toddler pre-school programming that relates to the things we've been talking about — the importance of a problem-solving approach in education, based on the individual interests and learning styles. This programming proposes that people learn by experimenting, by raising their own questions, putting those questions to the test and revising them as a result of their experience. This approach believes in the importance of a learning environment that supports curiosity and problem-solving learning. Key to this approach are educators who know how to guide learners with the right questions at the right time. The founder of these Italian early-years centers is a guy called Loris Malaguzzi who talked about children and their 100 languages.

Tai: 100 languages?

Charles: Let me read you what I consider one of the great poems about learning.

The Hundred Languages of Childhood

The child is made of one hundred.
The child has
A hundred languages
A hundred hands
A hundred thoughts
A hundred ways of thinking
Of playing, of speaking
A hundred always a hundred
Ways of listening of marveling of loving
A hundred joys
For singing and understanding
A hundred worlds
To discover
A hundred worlds
To invent
A hundred worlds
To dream
The child has
A hundred languages
(and a hundred hundred hundred more)
But they steal ninety-nine
The school and the culture
Separate the head from the body
They tell the child;
To think without hands
To do without head
To listen and not to speak
To understand without joy
To love and to marvel
Only at Easter and Christmas
They tell the child:

To discover the world already there
And of the hundred
They steal ninety-nine
They tell the child:
That work and play
Reality and fantasy
Science and imagination
Sky and earth
Reason and dream
Are things
That do not belong together
And thus they tell the child
That the hundred is not there
The child says: NO WAY, the hundred is there

—Loris Malaguzzi, Founder of the Reggio Approach, Centro Internazionale Loris Malaguzzi

Here is how the Reggio folks describe the importance of using these "languages" to help children learn. Let me read this to you:

Symbolic languages, including drawing, sculpting, dramatic play, writing, painting are used to represent children's thinking processes and theories. As children work through problems and ideas, they are encouraged to depict their understanding using many different representations. As their thinking evolves they are encouraged to revisit their representation to determine if they are representative of their intent or if they require modification. Teachers and children work together towards an expressed intent (Centro Internazionale Loris Malaguzzi).

Tai: Wow, you discovered all of this while Mom and I were shopping? This is good stuff. I really like the last thing you read, the part about teachers and children working together.

Charles: Why?

Tai: Because I love the idea of teachers and students sharing the responsibility for learning, working together to make sure we learn things. I had some Grade 12 teachers who are learning partners in my success. What a difference it makes.

Charles: Yes, it does. Malaguzzi called it working "together towards an expressed intent." One meaning of this phrase is that the learning outcomes of the curriculum can be met through many different individual pathways with those 100 languages being understood and acted on through a process of students and teachers in partnership. Pretty powerful, isn't it, Tai?

Tai: Yeah, I love the part about "understanding and joy" from the poem. That's one thing that great teachers do, make sure we are having fun while we learn. Why is that so hard?

Charles: It shouldn't be but some how we associate things like "play" and "joy" as anything but serious. But while education is serious business, it can be fun at the same time. This helps the serious business have an impact on learning. And look at other things in the poem, anything else you find interesting?

Understanding and joy in learning (Shutterstock photo illustration)

Tai: Yes, when he talks about some of the things that need to be avoided — basically bad teaching — like the need to "listen without speaking"? This Italian guy is so right. Sure, I need to listen carefully to what others are saying but I need to ask questions too. I need to tell the speaker or teacher what I am learning or sometimes question what they are saying…in a nice way of course. The idea that we should "think without hands" is also interesting. That's so silly, the idea that you can't think new ideas by doing things with your hands, like all sorts of arts and games. So, in Italy with these Reggio centers for pre-school kids, what happens when they go to "real" school?

Charles: You mean Grade 1? These pre-schools are run by local cities but the school system is run by the Italian government and is completely separate in philosophy and teaching methods from the Reggio early-years centers.

Tai: Does that mean that a child can be part of a really great start in pre-school with this great approach then wind up in first grade with the old fashioned, "I teach, you learn" stuff?

Charles: Yes.

Tai: Ouch! What about in Ontario?

Charles: Well, full-day learning for four and five year olds is now provided by the government along with elementary and secondary schools. So the same minister and ministry are responsible for both. The potential for continuity is there and I sure hope this potential is realized.

Tai: Is Ontario's philosophy the same as Reggio Emelia's?

Charles: Yes, in general terms, for the junior and senior kindergarten kids.

Tai: But not for Grade 1 and above?

Charles: Not yet! But it's possible we could see a change over time. It would be more likely in Ontario than in a place like Italy where there are separate governments in charge of the two "pieces"— pre-school and school. Tai, at this point of our conversation, how would you summarize what is effective for you, when it comes to the teaching and learning process?

Tai: Ok, sure. I learn best when I am allowed to learn *with* a teacher, not just *from* a teacher; when I learn from and with other students; and feel respected and understood for my talents and differences about who I am and what I already know. Basically, I want teachers "to get me", including my particular approach to learning, including understanding my learning disability. Also, it's effective for me when I am rewarded for my progress and supported when I need help, rewarded and encouraged when I take risks. I want clear and constructive feedback about how to improve. I want to feel good about learning from mistakes. I also want to feel safe in giving feedback to my teachers about what is working and what is not to help them help me. I want them to ask me for feedback and mean it. That would make us partners for my success.

Charles: Wow, Tai, that is pretty comprehensive and to the point!

Tai: Thanks Dad.

4 What Does Ineffective Look Like?

Charles: We've talked a bit about what makes education work for you and your peers. Let's turn it over and chat about what doesn't work. What does ineffective look like?

Tai: Well, I started our conversation about the good things by talking about respect. So I guess I should start with the flip side of respect.

Charles: Okay.

Tai: Most teachers I have had have been very respectful of me and other students. And I don't think that the ones who haven't really mean to be disrespectful. I just think they are not sure they know what to do when, well, you know.

Charles: You seem very reluctant to let it all hang out, Tai.

Tai: Well, I don't want to hurt anyone's feelings.

Charles: You don't want to be disrespectful, is that it?

Tai: Yes, exactly.

Charles: I understand and respect you for that. Just tell your stories in a way that keeps things anonymous. You have told me for so many of your young years that you want to improve education, so this is your chance.

Tai: Okay. Well, for starters, I have had teachers who never learned my name or the names of any of the students. "Hey you," after two months in a class of 24, just doesn't seem appropriate. And you remember that student we met in Bologna? He told us that after two straight years with the same teacher, she never learned his name and the names of the other eight students! Nine students and he was called "Hey you," for two years. And what about that teacher who asked another student "Who is that thing over there?" She was referring to me as "that thing"! That teacher had known me for months.

Charles: Some people just don't have good memories like that science teacher you mentioned.

Tai: Okay, then what's wrong with a name tag? Why don't some teachers even care to try? The one teacher I remember who never did anything to learn about me, actually yelled at students to lower their voices. Can you imagine that? She yelled at us when some kids were speaking as her way of asking us to lower our voices. That's a pretty big contradiction. She was teaching a subject that dealt with artistic things and she would say "This is good", "This is bad." She not only made some people feel humiliated but she also showed disrespect for her subject by treating visual arts as a black-and white-thing, never providing reasons for her "good" or "bad" labels. This had a big impact on me. I went into the course with a love and some skill in visual arts and I left giving up on it. The environment she created just made me feel that it was not worth it anymore. I might get back to art along the way but not in school. There are so many other subjects taught more effectively where I can continue to learn things that will help me develop. I also can use some of my visual-arts skills in other subjects.

Charles: Could this teacher benefit from your feedback?

Tai: She would if she cared about what we think. I am just not sure she would be open to it.

Charles: Maybe no one has ever bothered to sit down with her and explain.

Tai: Maybe she'll read this book because that's all I want —teachers to make it so that kids feel safe telling them about things that will help the kids learn better, in the same way they give us feedback about how we can improve. Telling us, "This is good" and "That is bad," without any more information, seems lazy and punishing. It certainly doesn't help a student learn.

Charles: We'll get back to this. Are there other examples of disrespect?

Tai: Oh yeah, I'm just getting started. Do you remember when I went to middle school and what happened with the swim teacher, Ms. J? On the first day of swim class, all of the girls are standing around the pool and the teacher asked, "How many of you girls have started your periods?" No hands go up. Duh! How many 12-year-olds are going to admit that in front of 30 others who are mostly strangers?

Charles: So you came home and shared this story with Mom and me. I remember. For you, it wasn't a big deal, just strange that she didn't send a note home or ask kids to let her know individually, if and when being excused for swim class was necessary. We discussed this and decided that the next time I was in the school, I would provide this advice to the principal. So I did. I didn't make a big deal about it. I just offered an alternative idea about how the teacher might better handle it so she wouldn't be under the impression that no 12-year-old girls are menstruating. The principal was very grateful for the advice and said she would coach the teacher accordingly

Tai: Well, the following week, things in swim class turned ugly for me. The teacher was rude to me, made me swim with the beginners when she knew I was a strong swimmer. And she just made my life around that pool miserable.

Charles: Yep, I remember. I told you to suck it up, be respectful and don't take it personally. I also raised this with the principal next time I was in the school. I asked her what I thought was a silly question. "You didn't tell Ms. J what specific student and parent provided the advice about how to handle the period thing, did you?" The principal answered, "Well, sure I did. Guess I shouldn't have, right?" Unbelievable! And this was an experienced principal who knew that our advice wasn't a personal complaint but general advice.

Tai: Exactly. What the Principal did was much worse than what Ms. J did, in my opinion. Ms. J may just not have known any better and the Principal probably turned it into a big deal. Ms. J got defensive and took it out on me. She shouldn't have but I understand how she might have felt.

Charles: And the Principal never apologized for this breach of confidentiality, at least not to me. Did she apologize to you?

Tai: Nope. But the whole challenge is that for things to work, everyone needs to be open to constructive feedback, to keep things positive and safe. Sure, Ms. J should have been mature enough not to take things out on me. The question is, did the Principal provide positive and smart feedback to Ms. J? If she did, then why did the teacher get so upset? I will never understand why the Principal mentioned that I was the source of the feedback.

Charles: You are right. Nothing will ever be perfect but people and organizations that learn how to give and receive feedback are the ones that are always improving.

Tai: But that wasn't the worst example of disrespect.

The worst time for me was when I was given inoculations that I didn't need, didn't want and I was forced to have them anyway because teachers and others simply did not listen to me. You remember, Dad? Because we had traveled before I got to middle school, I had already received shots for hepatitis. A few months before Toronto Public Health was to come to our school for the inoculation program, I brought home a form.

Charles: I remember. We were asked to fill it out and provide permission or explain why you did not need the shots. There was a section to fill out if you had already received the shots in question, when and where. I completed and signed the form stating that you did not need the shots.

Tai: Yep, I took the completed forms back to school and forgot about it. That is, until shot day arrived about three months later. My home room teacher, a really great person and teacher announces, "We're next for the hepatitis shots." So I tell Ms. G, "I am sure I have had these shots before," not remembering the details of that form months before. I tell her that I think I should call you and check. I tell her you always have your cell phone on. And she says, "Don't need to; all kids are supposed to get these shots," and she led us all to the lineup. So we line up and there are two nurses, one who is asking for our names and one who is the needle person. I give my name to the first one and tell her, " I think I have had this shot. Can I call my dad?" She says "Your name is on the list," but she checks with Ms. "Needles" and she says "If her name is on the list, no need to call her father." Ms. "Needles" sticks me and after school I call you to tell you what happened. I didn't know if there would be a problem getting the same shot twice and maybe I was wrong about having had this shot.

Charles: I remember the call, Tai. You were very upset. I told you that "yes," you had already had the shot but not to worry about any bad effects. That was a father's little lie, because I didn't know. But I called your doctor's office and spoke to the nurse to confirm that there would be no harm. The next day, I called Toronto Public Health, finally got through to the right person who called me back to confirm that they had made a mistake. They had the original form where I signed off on the box that clearly said you did NOT need the school-based shots. Three weeks later, I received a letter from the Chief Medical Officer of Health of Toronto apologizing with a clear description of what happened and what they were going to do to fix their systemic problem to prevent recurrences with other kids.

You can't ask for more, unless, I guess, what happened to you was a more serious error with more serious consequences.

Tai: But no one at the school has ever apologized, have they?

Charles: I took that letter to the Principal, told her what happened, explained that your home room teacher, someone you really like, and continued to respect regardless, didn't actually believe that you had already received your shot and didn't allow you to call me. I suggested that she might wish to use this as an example of showing respect for students, a lesson in listening to students more authentically. I asked the Principal to gently and respectfully chat with the teacher. I asked that it be put into the context that this wasn't an isolated situation; that too often, educators, including principals, simply assume kids don't know what they know. I actually suggested that they have a PA day when everyone talks about how to implement "respect" and that they use case studies like yours to illustrate the problem. The Principal took a copy of the letter, said "good idea" and since then, zero apology about what happened, and zero follow up.

Tai: Same on my end. My teacher never mentioned anything to me but continued to support my learning as she did with all of the kids. I mean, you're right. Ms. G. is a wonderful person. If Ms. G didn't listen to me, show me respect for my knowledge about the previous shot, and give me a chance to call you, then there is real problem with the word "respect" and what it really means.

Charles: I agree. The word "respect" is plastered all over every school, college and university as the key value that everyone is supposed to cherish as part of their missions. I wonder how often there is a professional development workshop for teachers at all levels on what behaviours coincide with respect? I know where I teach, most professors show enormous respect for their students, listening to their ideas and giving them tons of feedback to help them along.

Tai: Sure, but you teach PhD. students. They are all older, so it's different. But can you give me an example of disrespect?

Charles: There are a few professors who are not very good at providing feedback to students in a timely way. One disaster I can think of is a professor who did not provide feedback to a student on her draft thesis for over a year. The student had to pay extra tuition and her professional life had to be put on hold. And, in the end, even the quality of the feedback wasn't very good. The student finally came to me for advice after a year had passed. I told her to have a direct conversation with the professor and to provide the professor with a two-week deadline. She said, "Oh, I can't do that, that would be disrespectful to give a professor a deadline."

Tai: Not after a year of not hearing anything, it's not!

Charles: I agree, but we're talking about the power of position and authority. I advised her to either confront the professor or find another supervisor and dismiss the professor as her supervisor or take the case through the university's workplace-harassment process.

Tai: What's that?

Charles: If someone in a workplace feels that they are being abused by someone in authority — sexual harassment, verbal or physical abuse, things like that — they can request that an independent process look into the problem and resolve it. This protects people from abuse of power and authority. Ontario's workplace harassment and discrimination policy has its origins in a university when, many years ago, a professor was sexually harassing one of his graduate students. Anyway, the student I'm talking about found it really difficult to take on the professor in any way, so she waited it out, paid more money to keep her student status alive and finally received feedback and eventually got her PhD.

Tai: If adults find it difficult to give a teacher feedback, imagine how tough it is for kids. But still I have had so many teachers who make it easy to have conversations about how to improve the process of teaching and learning. I always hear you say, that "What is right is more important than who is right."

Charles: Learning should always be a shared experience, not just between a teacher and a student, but among and between all students, teachers, even the principal. And it should never be about, "I'm the teacher so I'm right," but occasionally it seems so.

Tai: I just love it when a teacher says to me or another student, "Wow, I never thought of it that way, thanks." This shows us that they are always learning too, and that they are prepared to learn from us. It must be difficult to pretend to know it all.

Charles: That's true. Pretending is one thing. There's hope for those who pretend, because there's always the possibility they will somehow, someday, feel secure enough to admit and embrace the notion they can learn from students. I worry more about people who aren't pretending they know it all. They actually think they do!

Tai: I understand what you're saying. Do you remember when I took an online course a few summers ago to see how I would do with e-learning? There were several assignments that didn't make sense; the instructions were confusing. So I sent the teacher an e-mail. In both cases, he wrote back with, "Hmm, you're right, I'll fix that and send out a blast to all of the students. Thanks, Tai!" Instead of "Just re-read the instructions, it will become clear what you have to do," which is what I have had from a few teachers.

Charles: That's a good example of how learning needs to be a joint, two-way process. Anybody who is teaching, training or coaching another person should be adapting and learning themselves. Sometimes it's a moment-to-moment thing with an individual student. Other times, it's a matter of paying attention to how all of the students are doing. For example, a teacher might give a test and discover that most of the students failed to do well on a certain part. An adaptive teacher will take this as important feedback and work towards improving their strategies in a certain area of learning. They adopt that shared approach to learning we've been discussing.

How do grades reflect on the teacher? (Dreamstime photo illustration)

Tai: What about final grades? Is it a sign of a good teacher if the grades are generally high, or a weak one who was too easy on students? Do some teachers like to grade tough to show others — the students, other teachers and the principal — that they are really good, smart and strict? What's with these different attitudes towards students and grades?

Charles: In my experience, there are teachers — and I am speaking about my direct experience with other professors and even some teachers that I had myself — who fit all of the categories of the questions you ask. My personal philosophy has always been to take responsibility for doing all I can to ensure students succeed. I personally think of myself as an enabler of learning, a facilitator and a partner with my students. When I was in government, we launched a Royal Commission on Learning, not "Education" because we wanted to emphasize the over-riding purpose — student learning. When I first became a teacher in Montreal at McGill University, my department chair called me into his office after my first semester of teaching and asked why most of my students got A- or higher. I explained my approach to teaching, including my grading system. I believed in being clear about the learning objectives and I gave lots of feedback to students with chances for them to demonstrate that they knew the stuff for the final project assignment and the course, I gave them an A- if they demonstrated all of the basics of the learning outcomes. I gave an A if they taught me something I didn't know and an A+ if I thought they should have been teaching with me.

Tai: What if they didn't achieve the objectives?

Charles: I gave them an "incomplete" and tons of feedback and they had six months to complete the course for a grade, as set out by the registrar.

Tai: What happened? And what did your department chair say?

Charles: As I recall, about 20 students got A-, eight received A's, and two students got A+'s. The department chair responded, "That's completely unacceptable. McGill has the best psychology department in Canada and we want to keep it that way." He said my approach lacked rigor, that I was too soft, too young to appreciate that I needed to challenge my students, and set higher standards.

Tai: What did you say to that?

Charles: I stammered a bit and tried to explain that my standards were high. I showed him the level of expectations, the specific learning outcomes and samples of the work. In other words, I provided what I thought was a solid case based on evidence not ideology. He didn't buy it and ordered me to "toughen up."

Tai: Did you? I can't imagine you ever giving in.

Charles: Well, I changed my grading system a bit, turned the basic achievement success benchmark as a B+ and went on from there. He never bothered me again. But I did give tons of feedback to everyone so they did learn what they were supposed to learn.

Tai: Why did you cave in?

Charles: I didn't have tenure. I was young and a bit insecure and I was on a kind of probation for my first three years. I also did something else that irritated him. I had students evaluate my teaching.

Tai: Why did that irritate him?

Charles: Because this was a long time ago and very few professors were asking for feedback from students at the time. He felt it was just a popularity contest. But I showed him the system and that it was a completely anonymous process that protected the students. Despite my explanations, he told me that what I was doing was turning over power to students, and who knows where that would lead. I was stunned. This was at the end of the 1960s when student power was already part of university life. The funny thing about this chair is that he was one of the best statisticians in Canada. He wrote a very famous textbook and was a person of logic and evidence. But when it came to teaching it seemed that he left his research mind behind. While we were in the middle of this discussion, I also asked him to compare what I was doing with what we academics do when we are getting ready to submit an article for publication. The process is that we ask other professors for feedback to help us make it better and we keep showing colleagues drafts until it's in good shape. Then we send it to a journal and if they like it, they will publish it or they give us feedback that will get it ready for acceptance.

Tai: That's what many of my teachers do —the ones who make the big differences. So did your department chair get what you were trying to say?

Charles: Maybe, but he seemed to think that what we do as teachers should be different from what we do as researchers. He was stuck in the old approach—"I am the teacher, you are the student. I will impart my knowledge to you. If you get it, fine. If you don't, it's not my responsibility, it's entirely yours."

Tai: That old "teacher is all powerful" approach is still around.

Charles: So, back to your original question. I do think that there are many who share the approach that your great teachers and we believe in — that it is about mutual responsibility and two-way feedback so that everyone succeeds. But I also think you are right, Tai, that the old model is still at play in too many places—schools, universities and colleges and even in the workplace. It is a kind of sink-or-swim approach. Well, sinking isn't going to help anyone, least of all those who drown because the system has let them down. But we shouldn't forget that many teachers are respectful; they want students to achieve, to learn and to enjoy learning.

Tai: That may be true, Dad, but then why do some teachers always show up late to class, give grades without any feedback, speak rudely to students and are teaching subjects they aren't trained to teach? It's not just about getting good grades. I want to know what to do better, what did I get right and why. I want to know what the grade—on an assignment or test or presentation in class — stands for.

Charles: So, don't your teachers explain the "whys" of your demonstrations of learning, those assignments, tests, and presentations?

Tai: Most do, but maybe 20% or so, don't.

Charles: Have you ever asked the 20% for more feedback?

Tai: Yes. And some of them give a bit but it's like pulling teeth. The ones who don't provide feedback in the first place just don't seem to care. You remember the story about my friend who gave a presentation in class and received a 70% with zero feedback?

Charles: Vaguely.

Tai: She went up to the teacher and asked: "Mr. W, the next time I give a presentation, what could I do better to improve my mark?"

Charles: What did he say?

Tai: He said, "Okay, I'll raise your mark to 87%." No kidding!

Charles: Really? No feedback, just an increase to the grade?

Tai: Yep, and she wasn't asking for an upgrade. She just wanted to know how to improve her presentation skills.

Charles: Well, that's one for the record books. Why 87%, not 80% or 90%?

Tai: Who knows, pretty weird, eh? He didn't provide an explanation, just seemed to want to be nice and end the discussion about grades when all my friend wanted to know was how to do better the next time.

Charles: Let's get back to teaching subjects that teachers are unprepared to teach. I know that principals often get stuck with situations that are not easily resolved because of last-minute challenges such as filling vacancies and because of school board rules about who is eligible and available.

Tai: Kids don't care about the school board rules. The way we look at it is pretty simple. Yes or no, does this teacher, or that one, know what they're doing. I have had teachers who are trained in one subject and are assigned to teach another they know little or nothing about. I had one course in which I learned absolutely nothing, because of this.

Charles: I can't believe you didn't learn anything.

Tai: Yeah, I learned you can get an A in something without learning anything.

Charles: I assume the Principal was just trying to make best use of the hand he was dealt.

Tai: That may be, Dad, but we're talking about my education, and that of my fellow students. My principal is a great guy and I think he's someone who totally gets what's best for kids but he does have these problems but then they become the students' problems.

Charles: You have something there. What about that team-teaching experiment where he tried having two teachers work with you and 31 other students? My guess is that he had to find a solution to a problem dealing with student numbers that didn't add up.

Tai: It was a total disaster. There were two really nice teachers, who never seemed to talk to each other or plan anything together and they gave us mixed messages about our work. I once got back a draft essay that each one had read separately. Each gave me specific feedback about changing a certain paragraph that contradicted each other. Not intentionally. but it sure confused me. I did figure out a way to write the paragraph to suit each of their suggestions but it was twice as long as necessary but they both seemed pleased with the result.

Charles: Did you tell them about the confusion?

Tai: Yes, but it didn't help, the whole course was like this: "Tai, why didn't you hand in your assignment. You are always early, never late?" I told the teacher I had given it to her partner a week earlier. "Oh, sorry about that."

Charles: Ouch. I like to team-teach, at least when the partners match and complement each other. I had a great experience a few years ago with a colleague who is completely different from me. But because we planned and worked well together, it seem to work for the students, at least that what our student evaluations said. But a long time ago, I once worked with a great guy, an incredible professor. He was very dedicated but totally absent-minded. I was home one night doing some reading and relaxing when the doorbell rang at about 7 p.m. I answered the door and standing there was a very famous Canadian professor, Northrop Frye. I politely asked him what he was doing at my place. "Oh, so sorry, Professor H. told me that the seminar you both conduct is taking place tonight at this address," he replied. "Oh, yes, on the 17th, correct, but it's taking place next month," I stated, adding "how well do you know Professor H?"

"Very well, sorry to disturb you, I completely understand."

Tai: Nice story, but what does that have to do with my dealing with my odd couple?

Charles: Well, just that sometimes two decent and smart people can get it right if they complement each others' strengths and weaknesses and work together, but also how folks can get it wrong. Besides, I always wanted to tell that story about Northrop Frye showing up on the wrong night and week. But let's get back to teachers and their knowledge of their subjects. So you had a few teachers who didn't have the background required. I assume that those were exceptions.

Tai: Maybe, but what about the substitute teacher problem? I think I had over 150 classes last year that were taught by subs. So we're talking about 225 hours being taught by subs. That's about two weeks of school if you subtract lunch. And with subs, the quality is really mixed.

Charles: Why do you think you had so many subs?

Tai: I don't know. I mean, people get sick at the last minute and you have to find someone to come in, I guess. And I think our school is really big on professional development so teachers need to take time off for special PD activities. I get that. I'm just saying that what happens during these sub classes can be quite funny, strange or sad depending on who you get. It's sad because sometimes you get people who are clearly beyond their best years. Then you get the ones who assume students are going to act out because that's what is supposed to happen with students and subs. So they come into the class with attitude. They act all tough and spend twenty minutes on rules, assuming all kids are bad. One of them sent me to the office because I told him I had to go take a make-up test. He didn't know a thing about me and assumed I was lying. He angrily told me to go immediately to see the vice-principal. He spent the whole class implementing his rules. There was no time for content. But some substitutes are really excellent. They are respectful, know their stuff and have some things we can do that are useful and fun for a class or two even if they aren't exactly sure where we are in the curriculum.

Charles: You said you had some funny experiences with substitutes as well.

Tai: Some of them use humour to keep it loose and relaxed. But the most outrageous example was the one who was most honest. "Okay kids. I don't know a thing about math so do whatever you want to do amongst yourselves. I'm going to be reading my newspaper and trust me, no math questions." This substitute thing is something that needs to be fixed, Dad.

Charles: I agree. One of the problems may be that teachers are allowed a certain number of sick days. Perhaps some of them take a sick day even if they're not sick. In many workplaces you'll hear some folks say, "I'm going to take a mental health day," to have a long weekend. Of course, some people are definitely stressed out by their workplace for a whole bunch of reasons. Have you noticed any connection between days off and your sense about whether a teacher is enjoying teaching or not?

Tai: Not sure, but you mean all a teacher has to do is tell the principal "I'm sick" whether they are, or not.

Charles: Well, yes. But let's assume that most teachers, any worker, would not abuse their sick days.

Tai: But what if some teachers are away a lot? How many sick days do teachers have each year?

Charles: Depends on what jurisdiction we are talking about, but anywhere from 15 to 20, even a bit more.

Tai: Well, that could be a whole month! What if some take most of these?

Charles: It would be up to the principal to have a chat to explore what's going on. This is a tricky conversation to have and takes a good deal of skill on the part of the principal because these sick days are part of the teachers' union contract. And of course, it was a big and sensitive issue in Ontario this past year.

Tai: I guess great principals have to deal with the individual differences of their teachers in the same way we've talked about how great teachers need to know their students.

Charles: Yes, that's it. In both cases it's all about leading through trust. My guess is that some principals might just want to avoid discussions that have some potential conflict lurking around the corner.

Tai: So they let students suffer because they don't want to deal with difficult things?

Charles: Not intentionally, but it is not uncommon for managers in any workplace to avoid conflict at the expense of others. But conflict in and of itself isn't a bad thing. It's how it's resolved that's key.

Tai: Before we move on, what do teachers' unions have to say about this kind of stuff?

Charles: I think you already know that I am a pro-union guy. Unions were formed because workers needed protection against unfair management behaviour. So unions exist to ensure that their workers are treated fairly when it comes to pay, benefits and working conditions.

Tai: Okay. But do unions protect the workers when they are not getting the job done?

Charles: Unfortunately, this is a problem. There should be more effective ways of dealing with chronically bad behaviour. My experience leads me to believe that people who are not doing well at their work already know it themselves. They are not happy and are stressed out.

Tai: Have you ever dealt with this kind of thing?

Charles: Yes, I have.

Tai: I'm listening!

Charles: My first experience of this was when I was a young professor. The secretary at the centre where I was working was a terrific person but a total disaster as a secretary. For two years, we all complained to the Director, "You have to get rid of her, she's messing up our lives, getting everything wrong." The Director was a really nice guy who hated conflict and avoided dealing with the issue until we all said, "It's her or us." It was that bad. He finally said, "Fine, I'll do it." A few weeks later, I was sitting in my office and the Director called me and asked if I would come and provide moral support to him while he told "W" she had to leave. I said sure and walked over to his office. He called "W" into the office. She sat down and the Director then said, "Charles has something to tell you."

Tai: You're joking.

Charles: No, he was so nervous about telling her she

wasn't up to the job after more than two years, that at the last moment, he passed it on to me!

Tai: What did you tell her?

Charles: I didn't have a lot of time to prepare, but I said, "We have really enjoyed having you around as a person, but when it comes to your secretarial skills, well, we need to have someone who can…" "You mean someone who actually knows how to do this kind of work?," she interrupted. I replied "yes" and she said, "What took you guys so long. I am a complete disaster at this job!" She laughed when she said this and asked if she had to leave immediately, to which the Director said, "Oh no, take your time finding another job," to which I intervened with, "Yes, let's say, two months from now at the latest, and we will provide you with proper severance pay. We will also help you find something more matched with your skills."

Tai: So what happened?

Charles: I volunteered to work with her on determining where her talents were. It turned out that she really liked to work with numbers. With our help, she got a job as a research assistant doing coding for a professor in the psychology department. She was at work at her new job within three weeks.

Tai: So, the moral of the story is, "Let's chat about how you're doing"?

Charles: I think some principals are great at building the trust with their teachers that allows for candid conversations but it can be difficult to move people into different positions, different subjects, or to encourage them to retire or leave to pursue something they would enjoy more than teaching.

Tai: Okay, now I'd like to ask you a question about the use of power by teachers. It seems that the great teachers never use their power to get us to do the things we need to do. While I know my great teachers have power over our grades and assignments and the like, most of them keep it in the background.

They just try to lead us by having a respectful relationship with us. But there are a few who make it clear all the time that they are in charge, with no room for a partnership with their students about their own learning. It seems that the bossy teachers find the classroom a nice place to take it out on students. It's not appropriate to pick on kids for no reason.

Charles: Kind of an abuse of power, Tai? I think I know what you mean. I have come across people like that. On a couple of occasions it turned out that, things were not going well for these people. In a few cases, they had real heartache in their lives, like a child who had died. Knowing about such private difficulties in the teachers' lives made me more understanding. It was easier to respond to their unfortunate approach with kindness or at least a good measure of understanding rather than anger or confusion.

Tai: Did it make a difference?

Charles: Yes, it did. If someone isn't having a good time of it and they are pushing other people away, sometimes turning the other cheek and ignoring the bad stuff can break the ice.

Tai: But it's not right or appropriate for students to be expected to be psychologists and social workers.

Charles: I'm not suggesting that. I do understand that there is not much you can do. That said, you might try to at least assume that a teacher like this isn't enjoying life as much as you are and try not take it personally.

Tai: Oh, I never take it personally, Dad, because the teachers I'm talking about are mean to everyone. But I understand your point. By the way, did you ever overuse your power as a teacher?

Charles: Well, I try to avoid it at all costs but I recently did have a situation where l lost it a bit. A few years ago, I was in a seminar with 16 doctoral students. This one student made a few comments that I thought were completely off base and unfounded. This student and I had done a lot of work together before he became a student of mine. In other words, we already had an established and respectful professional relationship. That said, I responded to his comments with full force, telling him why his arguments were weak. This is the kind of conversation we might have had over a beer before he became a student in my class.

Tai: How did he respond?

Charles: Fine actually. He came back at me, and we continued for a few minutes.

Tai: What did the other students think?

Charles: Well, that was the problem. Most of them did not know of our previous relationship and I am certain they found my approach both surprising and unfortunate. Actually, I know how some of them felt.

Tai: How?

Charles: Well, I apologized for being so forceful with the student, who in turn, explained that it wasn't a big deal and so on. I also sent an email that evening to all of the students apologizing further for my behavior; that taken in the context of the classroom, my approach was an example of me of "overplaying the professor card." In the context of a couple of colleagues having a chat over a beer, it would have had a different meaning. But the same frank exchange in a classroom setting could be taken as "rude" on my part. It's not appropriate to say to a student, or anybody for that matter, "Your arguments are weak." There are better ways to communicate. When someone has the power of position, what is said carries exaggerated meaning. If a shoe salesman says, "Your feet are big", so what? You might never buy shoes from him and you can walk out, or you can agree with him. But if your dance teacher says the same thing, ouch, that hurts, yes? She has what's called position power so what she says is magnified. And even though I had a relationship with this student outside of the professor/student situation, context matters. And I did make a mistake.

Tai: I think you are being too tough on yourself, Dad.

Charles: Let's move on. I have always felt that educators should be judged by how well we support those who need us the most. Earlier, you talked about the identification of your learning disability when you were in elementary school. So, why don't you tell me about how you feel about the supports you have had as a special-needs student.

Tai: Well, it hasn't been that big a deal, other than getting moved out of French immersion in Grade 3 and not seeing my closest friends as often as a result. I was upset about that at first. But I haven't felt badly about the learning disability and I have been doing really well in school since I was tested for the disability.

Charles: But you have had special supports.

Tai: Sure, my Individualized Education Plan (IEP) gives me the chance to have more time on tests or have alternative approaches to tests. I also get extra support from some of the special education people at the school. And most of the teachers respect certain things about my learning style and needs. The great teachers know their students and they support the differences between one kid and another. But the ones that just teach as if we were the same, well they're not great at caring about things like my IEP

What does ineffective look like? (Raffi Anderian/Toronto Star photo illustration)

Charles: Are you saying that maybe all kids should have IEPs?

Tai: I guess so. Never thought of it that way. Sure, why not? It would also be good if teachers in school would get together on things.

Charles: What do you mean?

Tai: Well, if a kid isn't doing well, maybe the teachers who share this student could have a little conference. The teachers could see if one teacher is doing something that is working. I don't know, it just seems that teachers never talk about how to organize things so kids don't fail.

Charles: What you're talking about is called a "case conference" in other settings. Everyone who is dealing with a person shares in the way you have described. Can you give me some examples from your own experience?

Tai: Well, when I was in elementary school and my learning issue was first diagnosed, the principal, vice-principal and my teachers were all working together to make sure things were consistent. It was going really well until all of a sudden, it wasn't. For some reason, the teachers stopped working together and things became inconsistent and confusing. Teachers were asking things of me that were contradictory. They were still nice and all that, just seems that things broke down.

Charles: What caused this?

Tai: The only thing that changed was Ms. P, the principal, left. She seemed to have been the one who made sure that things went smoothly and consistently along with the vice-principal. But then she left too.

Charles: Now I remember. Do you think principals make a big difference?

Tai: Of course! You know that they do, big time.

Charles: But why would the teachers change their approach, their behavior just because of a new principal?

Tai: Who knows, maybe the new one asked the teachers to do all sorts of new things on top of what they were already doing.

Charles: And you are right. I do believe that principals are difference-makers. They are the ones who can ensure that everyone is working together to support students. They are the "master teachers". It's not an easy job. How have things been going more recently, Tai?

Tai: Well, last year and every year at my high school, we have a few weeks when we are preparing for performances, with rehearsals every day after school. After all, it's an arts school. Seems like some teachers who are not involved don't pay attention to the overall school schedule and what else is going on in the school—like major performance weeks—when they assign project deadlines or schedule tests. It's a school with many great teachers but sometimes it doesn't feel like they're a team working for all of the students, together as well as separately.

Charles: But isn't the support you have had to accommodate your learning disability an example of teamwork?

Tai: Yes, for sure, Dad. As I said before, most but not all of my teachers seem to understand my IEP and give me the supports I need. But not all?

Charles: Okay, I think we've established how important the principal is to the smooth running of a school and how much a good one helps teachers co-ordinate their teaching and planning challenges. We'll come back to this, but now I'd like to ask you about the guidance you have received about course choices and planning for your post-secondary education or training.

Tai: There are some really good people doing guidance at my high school but you have to seek them out. It's been okay for me because you and I have done that but there are lots of kids who don't have the backup you've been able to give me. For those kids who don't get the guidance help they need, it seems like they just take courses at random and don't know what they're doing or why. It just doesn't seem like the guidance support is well-organized so that all kids get attention and help.

Charles: Anything else about guidance?

Tai: Well, I took this course called Careers that was really a bit weird but interesting too.

Charles: How so?

Tai: This course is a requirement to graduate so I guess it is there to make sure all kids get some guidance. I chose to take this course on-line because I wanted to experience what e-learning would be like. The process was pretty interesting. We had exercises, problems to solve, mini-quizzes, research requirements and instruction on how to produce resumes and cover letters for job searches. And although I never met the teacher, he seemed to go out of his way to present his personality to us so we felt like we knew him a bit.

Charles: So it really worked for you?

Tai: The teacher seemed to know how to make the e-learning work even though a lot of the content was a bit simple. He gave me good feedback on assignments and he responded well to feedback I gave him on things that weren't working for me. I talked to him about some things that were unclear and he made changes to the instructions and exercises, telling all the students that he had made a mistake and was correcting it.

Charles: Sounds like it was a great experience, Tai.

Tai: Well, despite all this good stuff, his feedback on my resume was inconsistent with the background reading we had been given and he was really strict about how a resume should be constructed, like there was only one way.

Charles: I remember and I agree that he was quite rigid and that the background reading you showed me, provided some room for creative flexibility. I thought your resume was first class. As I recall, you challenged him a bit on this.

Tai: Yes I did, and his response was friendly but he made it clear he was the teacher and I was the student. We're back to those power issues we have been talking about, Dad.

Charles: Overall, it seems he showed that he was pretty flexible in responding to your feedback.

Tai: But when it came to something basic about what we

were supposed to be learning — such as different approaches to doing a resume — he wasn't flexible at all. Nice but not flexible. The idea that he could learn something basic or important from a student didn't seem to fit for him. But the good thing is, I have a pretty good resume to use. I did it my way, shared it with others we know who hire people and they told me it was great.

Charles: I think you have just reinforced one of the biggest differences between effective and ineffective teaching. Those who are more excited about what they have yet to learn and less arrogant about what they already know, are the teachers who are stars. You have made this point many times in our discussions.

Tai: I think that's so, Dad. Some teachers just seem to be stuck in what they learned back in the day and are just passing it on. If we get the content, fine. If we don't, that's our problem. The teachers who are still learning, still experimenting with their subjects and their teaching, and want each of us to be successful, wow, do they make a difference! But I am curious about what principals and others can do to help those teachers who need help.

Charles: Okay, so no one is perfect but always room for moving forward, getting better. I know you're curious about these things. What excites me about your curiosity, Tai, is that you also have some ideas for making things better for all students, not just yourself.

5 Getting Closer to Perfect

Charles: So, Tai, it's time to talk about how to move public education closer to perfect. Where do you want to start this part of the conversation?

Tai: To me, the most important thing is for teachers to listen to what students have to say about whether their teaching methods are working or not for their learners.

Charles: Would you and your peers feel comfortable providing candid feedback to your teachers?

Tai: Most of us wouldn't, which is why teachers need to use methods that are safe for students. Teachers can use surveys that are anonymous so students can be really honest about what's working for them and what's not. There are on-line surveys as well.

Charles: Yes, I have used Survey Monkey for this kind of thing myself. I have been using more old-fashioned student evaluations for improving my university teaching since I started. Over the past thirty years, college and university professors have been using student surveys and other approaches. It is very common now.

Tai: So why are student evaluations common in colleges and universities but not in elementary and secondary schools?

Charles: It may be because post-secondary kids and their families pay a large amount of money directly to the institutions for their education and they feel it is important to get feedback for improving the "product."

Tai: But don't you pay for my education now, Dad?

Charles: Yep, through the taxes we pay.

Tai: So?

Charles: I agree with you but the payment is not as direct and maybe too many people feel that younger students aren't in a position to provide effective feedback to their teachers.

Tai: That is so wrong, Dad.

Charles: I agree completely, Tai. I think elementary school kids are capable of providing specific feedback on how things are working for them; and that it can be kept comfortable and safe for them and the teachers. We could be teaching kids the art of constructive feedback, something that all people should know how to do well. Did I ever tell you about the feedback circles I facilitated for four and five year olds when I was studying how best to foster early learning?

Tai: No, Dad, that's one story that got away!

Charles: With the permission of the early learning educators, we gathered around in the usual circle, sang a few Raffi songs and I simply asked: "So what do you love about being in this childcare centre?" Wow, did they respond. And, of course, I asked what they would like to see more of, less of and different. Their comments were very helpful. I did this a number of times. Children, even much younger toddlers, are constantly giving their parents feedback about what's working and what is not. We just need to ensure that all educators, from the beginning, pay attention to the unsolicited feedback and create chances to solicit feedback once and a while. The effective educators do this for sure.

Tai: Exactly. Getting back to us older kids, there could be many ways for students to provide feedback to teachers, not just surveys. Each class could have a small committee of students that the other students could talk to about how the class is working.

This committee could meet with the teacher during the year to discuss how to improve things if necessary or suggest some new ways of doing things that could be more fun and exciting.

Charles: Do you think most teachers would want to do something like this?

Tai: Maybe you start with the teachers who are open to something like this. Having these teachers act as the leaders, to show others how easy and safe it is for them and the students could work. We need to say to teachers that this is all about working together to make things really amazing for the students and their learning. Then maybe the teachers who aren't using student evaluations will feel left out and give it a go.

Charles: Your point about making it safe for teachers is really important. Anything that threatens teachers just isn't going to fly. Earlier you talked about how important it is for teachers to know each student. What can teachers do to get to know students on an individual basis?

Tai: Well, my very best teachers just naturally take an interest in who we are, our special interests and our approaches to learning.

Charles: But you have an IEP that provides each of your teachers with a profile of your learning needs. Do you think even the best teachers know these kinds of things for all of their students?

Tai: Maybe not,, but they should. All students should have an individualized education plan or something that helps teachers get a head start on knowing their students. Earlier you mentioned that there's lot of talk about getting kids ready for school but not enough about getting schools ready for kids. And I totally agree with you. I think there is too much emphasis on getting the content of a course stuffed into our brains. Teachers should begin by getting to know their students in the first two weeks of school. They need to learn what makes us tick.

Charles: How would that work?

Tai: There must be some creative ways in which schools could develop an orientation program that goes both ways. I think orienting the schools and teachers to the students is more important as a first step than the usual student orientation stuff.

Charles: Interesting ideas, Tai.

Tai: Thanks, Dad. Why can't schools and teachers learn more about how we learn best like my seventh grade teacher did with that multiple intelligence test? Why can't they find out what we already know about a subject so they know which kids are ahead on the content? They could spend more of their time as peer tutors helping those kids who need help. Remember the story about my Grade 9 geography teacher who asked us on day one: "What has nothing to do with geography?" Well, we couldn't stump him; we tried for a half hour.

Charles: What do you think his big question was about?

Tai: He wanted us to know that we already knew a lot about geography but didn't know it. Did I just sound like Yogi Berra, Dad?

Charles: Sure did, Tai, but I understand. He wanted to connect his subject with what you are interested in and what you already knew. And I suspect it was a way for him to get to know what you knew.

Tai: Exactly.

Charles: What else comes to mind with your orientation idea?

Tai: Why can't they make it easier for us to get to know the teachers and how they plan to teach? This would make it easier to switch teachers if the match between their approach and our learning styles doesn't work? Why can't we have the first three periods of each course for students and teachers to interview each other for 10 minutes to get to know each other? I'm just saying that getting the best matches between students and teachers should be the first and most important thing to happen each year. Each teacher could meet one on one with each student or even meet with two or three kids at a time to find out our interests and passions, how we like to learn.

Charles: Those are some really good practical ideas. Adapting to individual differences of each learner is the essence of a great teacher. Kids' motivation goes up and so much is learned as a result. There is something called "differentiated teaching" that attempts to deal with these individual differences but it doesn't capture the kind of relationship building that you are talking about. Reciprocal orientation is what we should call your idea.

Tai: Do you think there's really a school that would do this kind of two-way orientation?

Charles: I'm not sure. Maybe there are schools that already do this kind of thing. But I do know that there is a good deal of pressure on principals and teachers to get on with the content and the curriculum of a province or state.

Tai: Why? Where does the pressure come from?

Charles: Likely from the school boards who feel the pressure for their schools to do well on system-wide exams. But you are correct. The emphasis placed on covering the content rather than focusing on what would be best for helping effective learning is pretty widespread. But, sometimes you need to slow things down to catch up. If teachers can learn more about the individual differences of their students early on, they can adapt more effectively to each student and provide the best and most appropriate instruction. So taking the time at the beginning of each year, as you suggest, would be a good investment. The idea of slowing it down, taking the time for students and teachers to get to know each other as you suggest, will create more momentum for everyone. That's what I meant. So what else needs to happen to get closer to perfect?

Tai: Well, maybe it's too easy for the wrong people to become teachers.

Charles: Explain, please.

Tai: I'm not sure, but don't you think teachers need to be better trained, spend more time learning how to teach?

Charles: It's probably not just a matter of training but selection as well. As you said, sometimes the wrong people become teachers. Some things can be taught. But other things are more difficult to teach and train for—things like deep respect for others, what some call "people skills" or emotional intelligence. So you want to make sure that you take the time and develop methods to ensure that you select for certain attributes. I've heard some people describe teaching as a "calling". Those people believe that there is something deep inside them that makes teaching and student success a total commitment. Consider your Grade 9 geography teacher. He really likes kids doesn't he? He seems to want to know you on an individual basis and acts like a student want to always learn more about you and the other students and teaching in general.

Tai: I know what you mean! He's always learning new things about how to teach what he's teaching and he shares that with us. He is always learning and I think that makes him a naturally good teacher. He is just so dedicated to making sure we get the support we need to succeed. He volunteers to lead school trips and to guide us in some of our extra-curricular activities. He is also a really nice person who seems so happy with teaching, his family and life in general.

Charles: All of the things you have mentioned are things that are not easy to train for. Genuinely liking children, young people, wanting to know them as individuals and being a curious learner are things that become part of someone when they are very young, part of the environment created by their parents, other family members and early learning educators. I'm not saying, Tai, that people can't change, can't learn how important it is to determine how each student is different and how teaching strategies need to adapt accordingly. But having a passion for each student's success? Well I think it's best for our education system to get a head start by doing a great job selecting who gets into teachers' "colleges" in the first place. I think most teaching programs already try to do a good job selecting for those important qualities with interviews and references, but there is probably room for improvement regarding how those things are done. As well, it would probably best to have 30- minute simulated classroom situations where potential student teachers come to a group of students—all chosen for their abilities to create a real sense that they are a genuine class of 15 students — and the student teacher applicant is asked to do an extemporaneously assigned task with them.

Tai: Extemporaneously-assigned task? How about saying that in English?

Charles: Sorry. The potential student teachers would not know ahead of time what they would be asked to do. They might be asked to teach something or they might be asked to demonstrate what they would do the first time they met a new group of students. We're just brainstorming here. I'm just suggesting that we could improve the manner in which we select students for teacher training.

Tai: Wouldn't that selection approach take too much time?

Charles: Well, if public education is as important to society as we think, then it would better to improve on whom we select for training or we deal with the problem issues later on. You're the one who thinks teachers ought to get to take extra time to get know each student. Surely, we should take extra time to find out more and more about who we want to teach our students. Maybe there are other ways to do this and naturally we need to take into consideration the need to have a diversity lens for selection regarding gender, race and experience. The point is to ask how we can improve selecting for things that are difficult to learn during the teacher-training process and professional days. Do you agree?

Tai: Sure. How important are grades in getting into teachers' colleges?

Charles: Right now, it is very tough to get into teacher-training programs because there are many more applicants than spaces. So I think grades probably play a big role. Why do you ask?

Tai: Because I think that really smart people, students who are off the charts, 90-plus brainiacs, probably don't always make the best teachers. I think that people who get really high marks are probably doing really well with traditional teaching but may not be able to adapt to that wide range of individual differences we have talked about.

Charles: OK, this is interesting. How would describe "traditional" teaching?

Tai: The teachers have the knowledge and they spoon feed it to the students and students with great memories feed it back on exams.

Charles: That may be true with some kids in some kind of courses. But there are subjects like Physics that require high-level problem solving and thinking skills. Different aspects of English, including writing creatively, requires more than a good memory.

Tai: I guess what I'm trying to say is that whenever school — with all of its subjects — is really easy for someone, comes naturally, those people may not have an understanding of how to teach others who don't get stuff "naturally."

Charles: I get it. I have had this theory for years that those who became the greatest "teachers" were those who had to work a bit harder to understand how to do the things they later taught. For example, in sports, the best baseball managers, football and hockey coaches, by and large, were not superstar players. To be successful players, they had to really break things down and figure out how to be better. But rarely has a superstar athlete become a successful coach.

Tai: Exactly! That's because the superstar students and coaches and teachers just think, "Hey, this is easy, let's do it!"

Charles: But lots of kids like you, Tai, get good grades.

Tai: That's because I work hard and because of the great teachers I have had, I have done well. I was talking about my friends who get marks in the mid-90s and above who don't have to study!

Charles: I think you'd make a great teacher. I assume you also think that some of your braniac friends could also be outstanding teachers.

Tai: Yes, for sure. There would always be exceptions to what I am saying, especially if they had access to a teacher-training program that helped them get to know themselves better. But the point is that we agree that we need to select people to teach who really like young people, are happy people, and judge themselves by how well their students do, especially the ones who are not "naturals"; and they need to find out along the way, how the students think it's going!

Charles: Sounds like you would like to be part of the interviewing process to select folks for teacher training.

Tai: That's a great idea! I would love to do that. You talked before about the idea that people who were applying to a teacher-training program had to spend some time teaching real students.

Charles: Yes, they already do student teaching as part of their training.

Tai: I know that. I have had many student teachers in school but no one has ever asked my opinion about their teaching, how well they relate to students and things like that. They probably ask the real teachers how they did but if the real teacher is a dud, what do they know? Even if the teachers who are evaluating the student teachers are great teachers, why don't the students get asked to evaluate the student-teachers? It doesn't make sense, a real lost opportunity.

Charles: That's a good idea. You are back to the notion of student feedback, not just when teachers are teaching for real but as part of the process of determining if someone should be admitted to teachers' college in the first place or if if they should graduate once they are in teachers' college.

Tai: Yes. So, Dad, how many people are turfed out of teachers' college if they turn out to be just average or worse in their student teaching?

Charles: I don't know. I assume it is a very rare occurrence. So let's be clear. There are three aspects to finalizing the appointment of permanent teachers — selection into the training program; the training in a university; and the third one, I will get to later, ok? As you said, more time is likely needed for the training period in teachers' college. But increased time in a training program, by itself, won't change anything. What is done with the increased time it takes to become a teacher, is the key. Do you know that in Finland teachers have to have Masters degrees to be eligible to teach first grade and up?

Tai: So having a higher degree makes a big difference?

Charles: Not in and of itself. But in addition to really knowing their subject matter, they get extra training in how to foster the learning of others. As well, maybe because of the extra time commitment, it also acts as a deterrent to those who choose teaching because they aren't really sure what else they want to do in life. Maybe if you need to put in more and higher quality time becoming a teacher, it will attract those who have that real commitment and cause others to think twice.

Tai: So you think our teachers need Masters degrees?

Charles: I am not sure of that myself, but having a chance to do more actual in-class teaching under the mentorship of great teachers — real master teachers — is likely a step in the right direction. And these master teachers and the professors who run the teacher education programs need to be superb at giving feedback, and keeping the standards expected of the student teachers high.

Tai: So, if student teachers are better selected and they have more time to learn how to work with students with better supervision, will this make sure that all teachers are like Mr. E. or Ms. M. or the three Mr. Ls?

Charles: Well, it should improve things a good deal. But it is quite possible that selection will always be imperfect even if we do some of the things we talked about before. Even in the best of situations, where people are hired in all sorts of positions with incredibly thorough selection methods, the match between an individual and a job could still be quite imperfect, even too imperfect. In that case, the process of education should be one that helps bring out a clearer sense of what's within each of us. Remember that the word education comes from Latin and means to bring out someone's potential. With more time to teach and more time for feedback from experienced educators, the process of teacher training should further act as a selection tool, not simply an automatic entrance to the teaching profession.

Tai: Didn't we say before that some of the student-teachers should be failed?

Charles: Let's say that they should be selected "out of teaching." They should be given clear feedback about their prospects as a teacher. They should be told that their references from their professors and teachers who have observed their student teaching will indicate their weaknesses not just strengths. Perhaps, they should be told clearly they might wish to choose a different career path. Professors need to step up to the plate and be clear and firm regarding feedback to potential teachers.

Tai: Dad, we talked earlier about the fact that it takes some people more time to learn what's necessary. If they just had more time and good feedback, couldn't they become great teachers?

Charles: That's a good question. In some cases, for sure. This isn't all scientific stuff, Tai. But when it comes to respecting other people, having a passion for every student's success, being creative and curious learners themselves, these things are really difficult to bring about in adults, young and old. These characteristics become strong and natural habits at an early age. Which brings us full circle to the importance of early childhood education that toddlers and beyond receive — or not — from their parents and early learning educators. If you were to ask Mr. E or one of your Mr. L's or Ms. M about their early childhood experiences, my guess is that you would learn something special about their early years and how it shaped who they are today. That's the way it is; but it does not mean that people can't change some of the basics. It's just much harder.

Tai: Do you think there are enough of right kind of people for teaching?

Charles: Sure, and because right now in our part of the world, for the most part, there are fewer teaching jobs, it is a good time to be more selective about who gets in to teacher education programs, improve the teaching of those student teachers and improve what we do during their probation periods. Although "probation" is a terrible word. Maybe a different word should be used. Perhaps this time should be an induction or orientation period when teachers are finally given a real chance to do their thing. But it depends on what jurisdiction we are talking about because in some places, they are signed to a real job at the beginning. And in other places, probation means that if you don't perform well during this period, the school system can get rid of you without too much fuss.

Tai: So whether it is a real tryout period depends on which school system we're talking about?

Charles: Yes. In my world of universities, we hypothetically use a probation system. Generally, professors don't get tenure for at least three years. Then we become permanent if a committee approves of our work. This is a tryout period where we can demonstrate our research and teaching abilities before we get our job-for-life card.

Tai: And how well does this work?

Charles: Wish you hadn't asked. Not very well. The percentage of professors who do not get tenure is very tiny compared to the percentage who get tenure. This is out of whack in my opinion — and in my experience. We are not very good at giving timely feedback to each other about how we are doing and once we get to know each other and become colleagues and even friends, we just don't have the courage to make the tough decisions often enough. As a result, too many students get taught poorly and the quality of academic scholarship suffers.

Tai: How many professors get this tenure thingy that shouldn't?

Charles: I have no idea but in my experience at three different universities, it's probably small in number but huge in impact. Maybe 10% or so should not be given tenure and the culture of sloppiness around these decisions is so prevalent that when a decision is made to deny tenure, all heck breaks out. There have been university presidents who have been driven out of town because they supported rare decisions to deny tenure. If we professors brought the same rigor to decisions about who gets tenure and promotions as we apply to our research, universities would be that much better and students and society would benefit much more.

Tai: But what's this got to do with teachers? Should "tenure" be something that takes three years for teachers to achieve in all school systems?

Charles: I'm not sure three years would be necessary. Perhaps two would be fine. What is key is that new teachers be given excellent mentorship from the great teachers, constructive feedback from principals and students according to your ideas, Tai, and when it's time for a final decision, it won't be a surprise if they are permanently hired, or not. And for the tough decisions to deny tenure, it won't be as hard because of the ongoing feedback the teacher has received. Did I ever tell you about the time I was told by my last baseball manager that I wasn't going to cut it as a professional baseball player?

Tai: Nope, another one of the few stories that got away.

Charles: I already knew from my performance that I wasn't good enough to go on and before he could tell me it was all over, I said, "What took you so long." Better to know earlier than later that it isn't going to work out than to go down a road of misery.

Tai: But won't some principals still take the easy way out?

Charles: By easy way out, do you mean hire the person even if they aren't great teachers? Good point. But we need to create a culture where the easy way out is to imagine life with the kind of great teachers you have talked about who do make it easy for both students and principals. And we should talk about the selection and training of principals too. My impression is that it is really hard to make the choice to avoid making a teacher permanent. With the union contract rules in many jurisdictions, it takes a huge amount of effort for a principal to make a successful case for dismissing clearly ineffective teachers. It's a fact and it's too bad, which is why a smarter and tougher process for training teachers and creating a genuinely effective try-out period is so key. But I think there is much more that could be done by principals, and those who lead principals, to enable the progress of teachers' improvement, especially those who are struggling. And maybe we could reduce the number of seriously ineffective teachers to a very small number. You know my friend Michael Fullan?

Tai: Of course I know Michael.

Charles: Well, Michael's latest book talks about the importance of a kind of collective professional development to overcome teachers' going it alone behavior.

Tai: Like their classrooms are their castles and they are the kings and queens.

Charles: Yes, exactly, and the draw-bridge around the castle only comes down to allow students to enter and leave.

Tai: So what's Michael's solution?

Charles: He believes that professional development should involve all of the teachers in a school, a kind of collective approach to supporting each other's progress as teachers.

Tai: You mean like PA days?

Charles: No, not at all. While some PA days are terrific, Michael and his co-author Andy Hargreaves, are referring to what happens on a daily basis. He thinks principals need to create a culture where all teachers are learning together and learning from each other; to create a culture where it is common for teachers to meet to discuss different approaches to teaching or how to best support various students they share in their respective courses, as you were suggesting earlier. Many people who write about education talk about how independent teachers are. They are in charge of their classrooms and in charge of their professional development. Great teachers, as you have said, keep on learning and experimenting. And while they seek others' advice, they pursue their ongoing learning largely on their own. Teachers who are not doing so well also seem to be on their own and perhaps in a lonelier way. Michael and his co-author quote another expert — Jean Rudduck — who said: "Education is among the last vocations where it still legitimate to work by yourself in a space that is secure against invaders."(*Professional Capital: Transforming Teaching in Every School*, pp.106, Teachers College Press, 2012).

Tai: That's interesting. But would some of the teachers who feel alone and who are not doing well as teachers really want to learn from other teachers?

Charles: I think they are more likely to learn from other teachers if it is done in a safe and friendly way than by being told they need to shape up by a principal who is getting lots of pressure from parents and students. And Michael's book gives us a promising description of how this could work. You should read it. Importantly, it should be mandatory reading for those who run training and selection programs for principals.

A culture in which teachers learn together (Toronto Star file photo)

Charles: So, Tai, let's move on to the next topic. How can you summarize other things that teachers need to be trained to do?

Tai: As I've said, my very best teachers are respectful. They take the time to know us, and they give us clear feedback about how to do better as well as the support we need to improve. They are also clear about what we are doing well and why.

Charles: The clarity of feedback is key, isn't it?

Tai: Yep. It doesn't really help me if I get 92% on an essay and I don't know why. As you know, I have had this experience. The great teachers really understand that tests, projects and essays are chances to learn if we have a good understanding of what we did well and why and what we didn't do well.

Charles: And speaking of feedback, maybe teachers who are struggling would benefit from feedback from other teachers if the environment were supportive and safe for this to happen, the kind of thing Michael Fullan is talking about, and why. Anything else?

Tai: I've said this before but teachers need to learn how to do these things and they need to know their subjects. It isn't enough any more to parachute teachers into subjects they're not prepared for. I have had just too many teachers who just do not have a clue about what they are teaching. And it sure makes a difference if they love what they teach. That is just wrong. And the Finland story you told me is good because, as you said they make sure that teachers really know the subjects they are able to teach.

Charles: True, Tai, content is important but you have also said that how teachers teach is more important than what they teach.

Tai: I really think that learning should be fun, should be about solving problems, working with other kids, and we should be able to do things that relate to our interests as we learn what is in the curriculum.

Charles: When you talk about solving problems, I assume you mean that you prefer to be an active learner rather than a passive one?

Tai: What do you mean by that?

Charles: You talked about the science teacher who put notes on the board and asked all the students to copy them into your notebooks. That's a kind of passive learning, just sitting there with the teacher who takes notes from her notebook, transfers them to the board and then asks you to copy them.

Tai: Yeah, what a waste of time that was. Why not just hand out the notes and give us a chance to play around with science like my other science teachers, like Mr. L?

Charles: Yes and, teacher training should teach future teachers how to adapt to the things that make each student unique as well. They need to know how to use teaching techniques that are fun, relevant to kids' interests and active. And they need to be able to provide quality constructive feedback. That's what I understand you are recommending.

Tai: You got it.

Charles: I haven't really talked about the early learning curriculum we developed in Ontario. It's an exciting play-based creative problem-solving environment for four and five year olds. The kids are working at various play stations, like water and sand tables. It is about active inquiry.

Tai: I remember when I was in kindergarten. We got to play a bit once in while, not a big deal. But in day care before I got to kindergarten, I can actually remember having so much fun playing with other kids. I am sure I was learning, getting my small brain to exercise.

Charles: Indeed you were, Tai. Now kindergarten in Ontario is full day and creative problem-solving and projects that come from the children's imagination have been developed, and are key components of the approach.

Tai: You mean the teachers don't decide what's going to happen and lay it on?

Charles: The teachers are there to set up the environment to apply a framework that encourages active and curiosity-driven learning and the guide the kid's learning; but no, it is not a top down, here-is-what-you-are-learning-today approach. Many of the ideas of this approach come from that Reggio Emilio place I told you about.

Tai: So what happens to the kids when they get to Grade 1 after they have been playing and learning by solving problems?

Charles: Good question. Oftentimes what happens in Grade 1 and beyond is what we call Drill and Kill, where students are taught content and tested. My hope is that all of us involved in education — from the youngest to the adults in my PhD. courses — are actively engaged in creative problem-solving work, and on really fun and meaningful projects.

Tai: Good luck with that! What's the "kill" part mean in Drill and Kill?

Charles: I think it means that the traditional approach kills creativity and independent learning.

Tai: It sure does.

Charles: People talk a lot about lifelong learning. So the challenge for all those who endeavor to support a real lifelong learning approach is that from the beginning, the learning opportunities must build on active learning, creative problem-solving and those individual differences of the learners we have discussed so often.

Tai: Yep, I get the need for learning to be all about individual differences of each student or learner. We've mentioned this as key to great teaching throughout the book. But not sure I get this lifelong learning thing.

Charles: Imagine a four year old at a water station observing the overflow of water as a result of her pouring liquid from a larger container into a smaller one, then adapting as a result when she tries again. She's experiencing the principle of "conservation of matter" and other related notions of science. Her highly elastic brain is taking it all in. At its most basic level, how different is the process of discovery from a professor of bio-chemistry experimenting in her lab? In between the opportunities of our youngest learners to express their curiosity in an unfettered manner and the opportunities of a professor guiding doctoral students, we need to resist the pedagogy that often seems deliberately designed to stifle the problem-solving and creativity we so desperately need to foster.

Tai: So you're saying that the kind of teaching going on for little kids should be the same for all?

Charles: Yes, exactly.

Tai: Were you also saying that the one-fits-all crammaramma approach is destroying kids' creativity?

Charles: Cramma-ramma?

Tai: I mean an approach that tries to cram content into our brains no matter who we are and no matter how we learn and no matter what we already know and no matter what our passions are?

Charles: Got it. Cramma-ramma? Very elegant way to describe what I meant, Tai, and yes, I think this stunts creativity.

Tai: Well, I agree with what you are saying. I talked earlier about how the really bad teachers I have had just turned me off thinking positively about the subjects they were teaching. And I know I need to get over the bad teaching so I don't throw away the benefits of those subjects. It's a shame, but it only takes one teacher to turn a kid off a subject or even school. And the great teachers I've had do the opposite — getting me interested in new subjects

Charles: I should also add another issue into this discussion. I know there were times when you complained about having too many students in your class?

Tai: Yep, sometimes over 30.

Charles: Well, it may seem odd, given all that we have discussed about the need for teachers to know about all of their students, but as we discussed before, class size is less important than pedagogy — the way teachers organize the environment for learning.

Tai: Aren't they both important?

Charles: Yes, they are but as I have mentioned to you, you can do some creative things as a teacher to foster excitement about learning and student success and enjoyment no matter how large the classes. Small group-project work and peer tutoring are good examples. Class size shouldn't be an excuse for teachers to give up on experimenting with ways to ensure active student learning and problem-solving.

Tai: I guess so but I have to think that great teaching and smaller classes are still best.

Charles: For sure. Anything else?

Tai: As I have said, I really do well with teachers who continue to learn about things themselves and their subjects, and who work on how to improve their teaching, things like that. When teachers are experimenting with new things, there's just something fun about it, kinda like they are the opposite of the know-it-all types. The other thing that the education system doesn't seem to understand is that kids in my generation are coming to school with a history of doing stuff on computers, loving the internet and Facebook. Then we get to school and they lecture to us. It's crazy. A teacher taking her notes, putting them on the board and asking us to take down the notes! Why don't we just get the notes online, and read them at home so when we are with the teacher, we can discuss or solve problems, and get new information on our computers?

Passive learning (Photo.com photo)

Charles: Not all kids have computers, Tai.

Tai: Most kids now have some access to computer, at school or libraries at least. And while many of my teachers have been great about the problem-solving and project stuff, even they don't fully understand the fact that we are digital kids.

Charles: Okay, but all of the good teachers you have discussed are probably still limited by the vision or resources of the school board. There are some outstanding schools and boards that have embraced technology and are doing innovative things. But you are right that we need to do more. We need to ensure that there is a learning revolution and it should start with how faculties of education organize the training of tomorrow's teachers. And I guess you would put at the top of the list for teacher training, the need to seek feedback from students on an ongoing basis.

Tai: Yep, I guess that's the most important thing. Remember when I told you about camp a few summers ago when I was a Leader in Training? During the month I was an LIT, my supervisor asked me and the others LIT's: "How is this working for you? Are getting enough support from me? Anything I can do to improve the way I support and help you?" She did this twice in that month. She called it a "check-in." All teachers should do this at least three times during a course. And those that are in the business of training teachers need to make sure they select people who listen to others, including students. There are different things a teacher can do to make it safe for students to give feedback. But teachers should create trust with each student so that even shy students will advocate for themselves. As a matter of fact, Dad, that should be the goal of all teachers—to make shy kids feel comfortable in advocating for themselves.

Charles: That is really well said, Tai. Let's talk a bit more about self-advocacy. Were you always good at it?

Tai: No, not at all. But there were some teachers who made it easier and, of course, when things got really awful with a few teachers, you advocated for me.

Charles: But we discussed earlier that some parents tell their kids to "just suck it up" and do their best even when it's clearly not working for them. I was also upset, as you know, , when I thought other parents were going to bring some tough feedback to the principal and it turned out I was the only parent who raised the issues about the teacher in question.

Tai: Yeah, even parents are afraid to advocate when things are not going well. They are afraid of the conflict coming back to hurt their kids. I really think those who train teachers should teach future teachers how important it is to reach out to parents, to make them genuinely feel like partners in supporting the learning of the kids they share. Teachers need to know how to do this! We need to move from parents trying to figure out how to advocate for their kids to becoming respected partners with the teachers.

Charles: Great point Tai. Parents and teachers need to deeply respect what each one knows about the children/students. The idea is the power of a three-way partnership for success among students, parents and teachers, right?

Tai: Exactly.

Charles: So we are back to the selection and training of teachers and principals. If you were in charge of training teachers, what other things do you think should be part of the teacher-training curriculum?

Tai: You know that poem from Italy and Reggio Emilia and the 100 Languages of Learning? I would want every teacher to get that training so they can learn to understand how to reach out to different kinds of kids. I would like kids at a young age to be able to learn more about their own approach to learning in the way that Ms. M did in with that multiple-intelligence process.

Charles: If you could wave a magic wand and bring it down to a few things that all teachers need to be selected and trained for, what would they be?

Tai: I guess I would say that their training needs to go on for all of their working lives. Great teachers, as I have said, seem more excited about what they don't know than being over-joyed about what they already know. I mean, while they love their subjects and create enthusiasm about what they are teaching, all teachers should be very eager learners.

Charles: I agree. The best teachers are lifelong learners. They are professionals and one key aspect of being a "professional" is the need to keep on keeping up by always learning new things. This is expected of doctors, lawyers, nurses—all those who claim to be in a profession.

Tai: And they need to really know their stuff. I have said throughout our conversation, that teachers need to know their students individually and make use of this knowledge to create flexible ways for each student to learn the curriculum. And so that teachers can do this, the professor types who teach future teachers, need to get this individual difference stuff and they need to treat the student-teachers in the same way. In other words, the professors need to teach this approach by modeling it themselves

Charles: You want professors who teach future teachers to practice what we're preaching? What a great idea! Naturally, that would require a major overhaul to teacher education and would require a major investment in the professional development of many professors. You think teachers work alone and are protected by the isolation of their classrooms? We professors are the original lone rangers!

Tai: Well, that has to change, right, Dad? Yes, the profs need to do what we said great teachers do, including that orientation idea where the professors would spend some quality time getting to know the student-teachers right at the beginning.

Charles: Your "reciprocal orientation" idea?

Tai: Yes, if we have to give it a fancy name, Dad. But everything we have discussed should be true for the selection and training of principals too. They should be outstanding at all of the things we have talked about.

Charles: I agree. They should be master teachers, coaches and they should model the seeking of feedback by seeking feedback from teachers and parents about their own leadership.

Tai: And from students too. I know Mr. S, my principal, seems open to feedback about how things are going and he makes it pretty easy for most of us to speak to him. But even Mr. S doesn't seem to have control over some things that are really important.

Getting Closer to Perfect   87

Charles: Like what, Tai?

Tai: Like who is hired to substitute. Like who gets to teach what. I have had too many teachers that just don't know how to teach or don't know how to teach a certain subject.

Charles: Yes, sometimes principals are hampered by the rules of the school board or by union contracts that make it difficult at times to hire the right people for the right jobs and the right time.

Tai: I think that principals should have more power to make these decisions. If principals are well-trained and selected, shouldn't they have the right to hire and get rid of teachers, and reward the great teachers? And shouldn't they be in charge of improving everything that goes on in the school, especially the improvement of teaching? Teachers need to be a real team—helping each other when it comes to supporting students, like you were saying before, the kind of approach that Michael Fullan was talking about in his latest book. We've talked about teachers giving major assignments at the same time or at a time when there is a school play or concert scheduled where some kids have performances for three nights in a row. That's the easy part to fix, but a team approach would really be great—every teacher supporting every teacher for the sake of students' success.

Charles: Yes, principals need to ensure that teachers, however great they might be, don't become "islands." To achieve that. the principal needs to develop the team approach we've been discussing. We need principals to ensure that they have appropriate professional development both for themselves and their teachers., They need to build a culture of common values, a kind of collective professional development on top of the individual PD that teachers and others need.

Tai: Right! Good principals can make a huge difference.

Charles: Tai, any final thoughts?

Tai: In thinking about the idea of providing the right supports to students so they will be successful and enjoy learning, I wouldn't want anyone to think that all students should be successful all the time on every task or project. I think it's okay to make mistakes even fail, as long as the failure is a chance to learn something through effective feedback. Failing in a positive environment can be a great chance to learn.

Charles: Failing in a positive environment is a great way of putting it, Tai!

Tai: Thanks, Dad.

Charles: Yes, you made that clear in our conversations. It's important to take risks, make some mistakes and learn from them, rather than just being punished. We want people to be resilient, to be able to bounce back from a setback with the confidence to learn from experience. And all of this can begin at an early age with parents who know the difference between risk and danger. So what's your biggest hope for this book, Tai?

Tai: My experiences are just my stories, no more than that. And while I think my stories may be much the same as those of many other kids, I want parents, teachers and principals to listen to students' stories, to really respect that we know what works and what doesn't when it comes to our own learning. All teachers and principals need to be really good listeners. Listening to us about what's happening is the best sign of real respect. I think too many parents tell their kids to suck it up when things aren't going well. Sometimes that advice is good. But often, parents need to listen to what their kids are saying and advocate for them. They need to teach their kids how to eventually advocate for themselves, too, like you and Mom did for me.

Charles: What about student responsibility?

Tai: Our job is to show up for classes, complete our homework on time and work hard and smart to get it right, and to ask questions when we don't understand something. I think we also need to be given a safe and frequent chance to say what is working and what is not working for us. If that can happen, we definitely have the responsibility to speak up in a respectful way about how things could be better.

Charles: So that last part of your responsibilities, Tai, depends on being allowed and even encouraged to express yourself about improving learning conditions in a constructive way.

Tai: Absolutely. There aren't many of us who have the nerve and the skills to self-advocate unless it is part of the culture, unless it is really considered a positive thing to do by all of the teachers, not just the great ones.

Charles: You have become a pretty effective self-advocate, and now that you are in your last year of high school have things become even more positive for you?

Tai: I think so. The older I get, the more control I think I have over what is good for me in school. I think I have learned how to ensure that I choose excellent teachers who demonstrate respect for who I am and how I learn. My Grade12 teachers are amazing. I think it would be great if students had the know-how and confidence to be better self-advocates earlier.

Charles: It seems to me, thinking back on our conversations that the thing that runs through all of them is the notion of mutual respect and for the importance of great public education; respect for the critically important role that teachers and principals play and the process that selects and trains them; and ultimately, genuine and deep respect for each student. With that kind of respect, the ongoing experiences of all students would be valued, evaluated and acted on to provide each student with an individualized learning plan with their success and confidence front and centre.

Tai: And I really hope other kids will write and publish their own stories so that eventually every school will be a place where all kids and their interests and strengths are really valued, where learning is radically fun, and everyone — students and teachers — are always getting smarter because they value giving feedback to each other because they are partners in learning. On top of that, parents need to encourage their kids to tell their stories and listen carefully to thveir kids' ideas and experience. If this can all happen, we will get much closer to perfect!

Under the right circumstances, students can soar (Toronto Star file photo)

Acknowledgments

Naturally, we are very grateful for the great teachers who have enriched our lives through their understanding, respect, commitment to our success . . . and patience. We are both eager students and look forward to continue benefiting from others from whom we can continue to learn.

To our colleagues at the Toronto Star and Wild Element getting this book "out there" for you to read in a timely and effective way is due to their expertise.

Finally, to Tassie Notar, a deeply valued moral mentor . . . and an even better mom and partner . . . we offer our deepest love and respect.

TPN & CEP

TAI PASCAL NOTAR is a Toronto-based grade 12 student whose interests include equestrian activities, hip hop dancing, photography, events management and journalism, having already published two articles for the Toronto Star. Tai has demonstrated her leadership skills both in school and in her role as a riding instructor and counselor at a summer camp for the past two years. Tai will be going on to Ryerson University to study Image Arts.

CHARLES E. PASCAL is an internationally recognized educator with expertise in early and higher education. A former college president and Ontario deputy minister, Charles was the Special Advisor on Early Learning to the Premier of Ontario when he wrote his seminal report, With Our Best Future In mind. Charles is currently Professor of Applied Psychology and Human Development at OISE/University of Toronto where he is coordinator of the Flex-time PhD. Program in Early Learning.

CPSIA information can be obtained at www.ICGtesting.com
Printed in the USA
LVOW01s1551091013

356187LV00013B/25/P

9 780991 972708